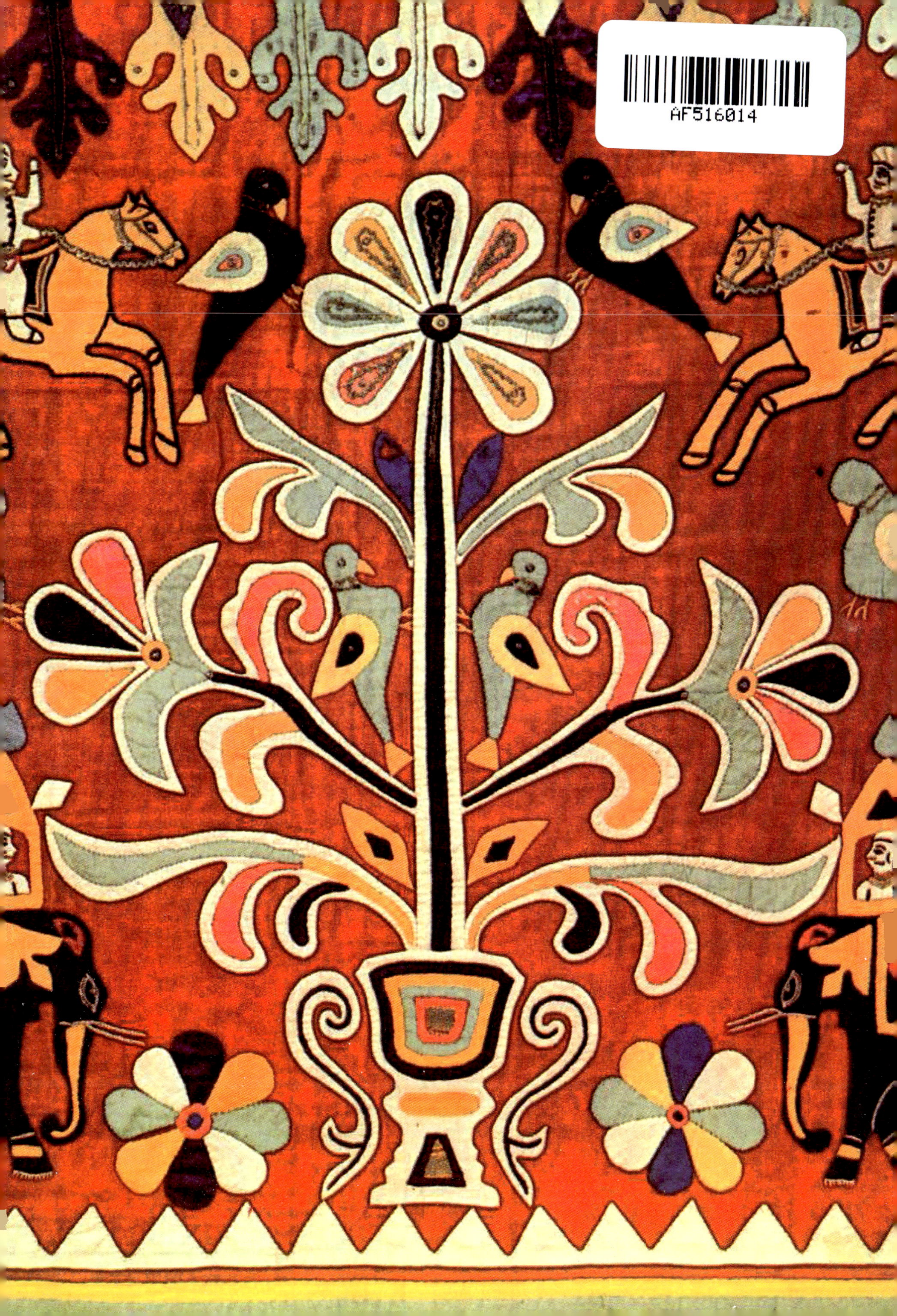

Megha Meets Vishwakarma

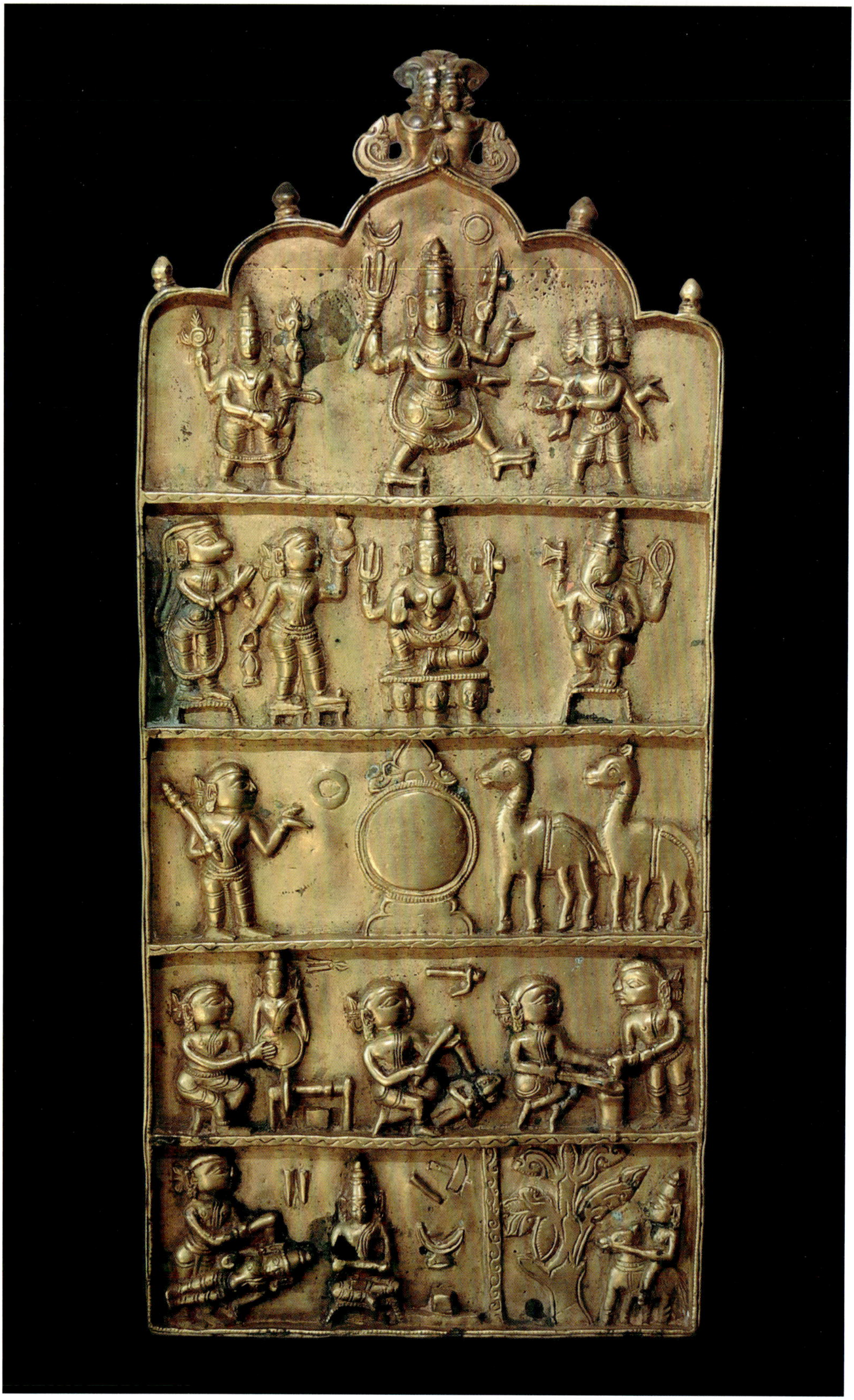

Vishwakarma plate, Andhra, 18th century

Megha Meets Vishwakarma

The Story of Indian Crafts

Harsha V. Dehejia

NIYOGI
BOOKS

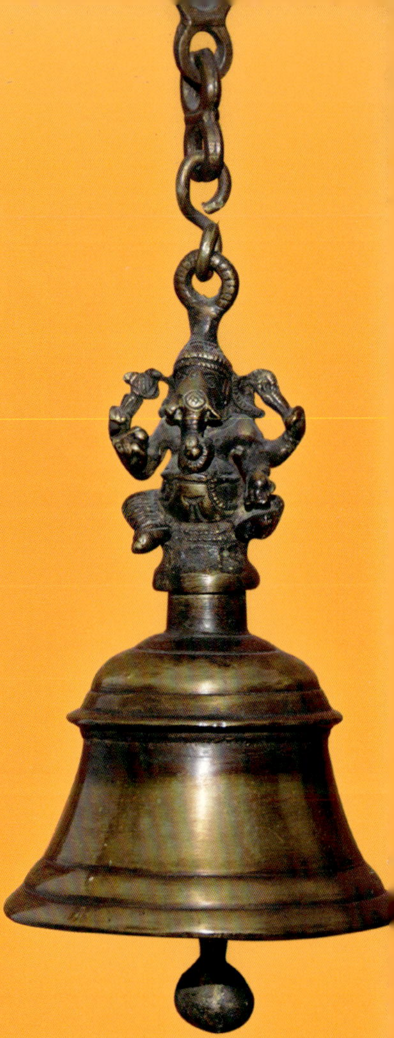

Published by
NIYOGI BOOKS
D-78, Okhla Industrial Area, Phase-I
New Delhi-110 020, INDIA
Tel: 91-11-26816301, 49327000
Fax: 91-11-26810483, 26813830
email: niyogibooks@gmail.com
website: www.niyogibooksindia.com

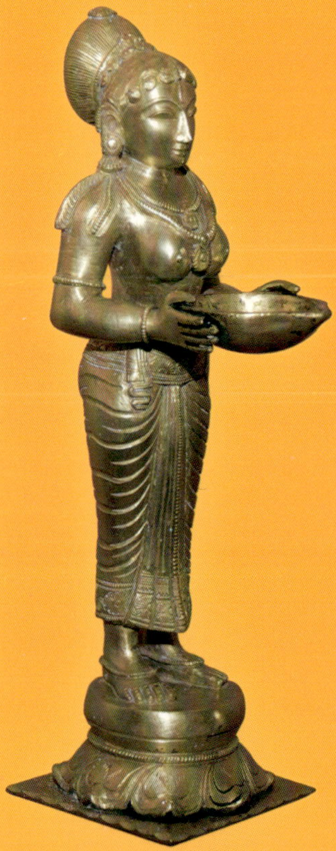

Editor: Siddhartha Banerjee
Design: Paul Crupi, Shashi Bhushan Prasad

Art consultant: Varsha Mehta
Artists: Vijay Sharma, Parikshit Sharma, Hukam Chand, Harish Raut

ISBN: 978-93-83098-36-1
Publication: 2014

Printed at: Niyogi Offset Pvt. Ltd., New Delhi, India

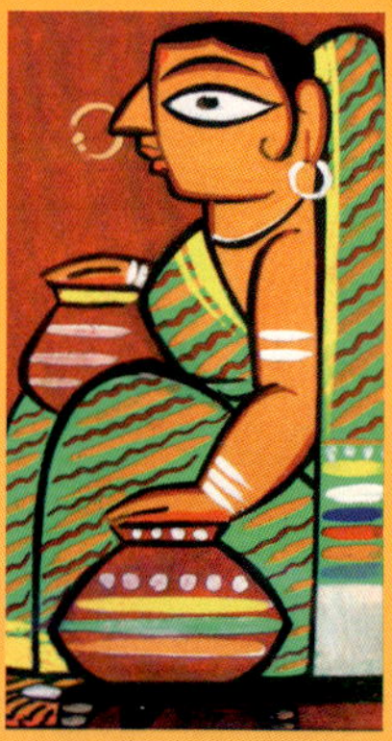

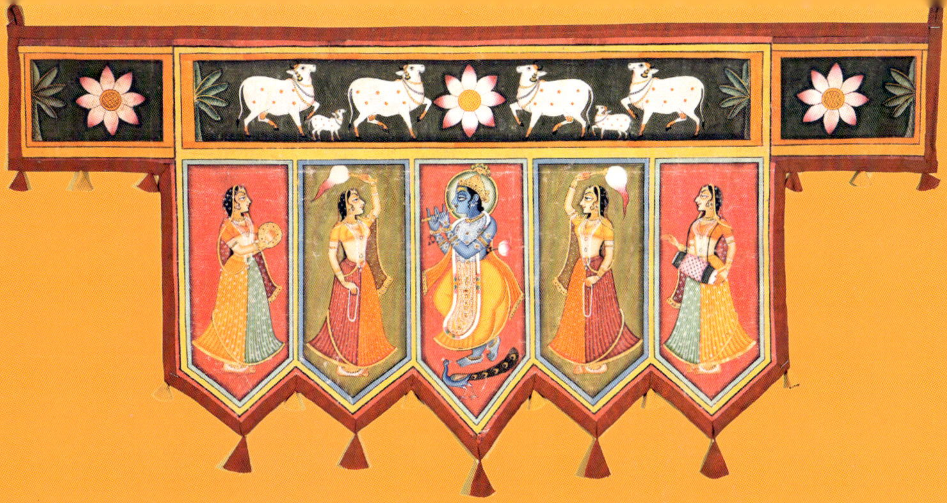

Dedicated to
the potters and poets, artists and artisans
shilpis and chitrakars
in whose minds there is an ancient memory
and in whose hands there is an earthy rhythm
who craft beautiful objects
to be in the midst of these is to be assured of
archetypal symbols, living myths and timeless metaphors
of well-loved designs, evocative colours
and cosmic shapes
and as we surround ourselves with their creations
we are touched by their beauty
and our daily life is filled with grace and dignity.
Come, join me in a journey
of Indian crafts.

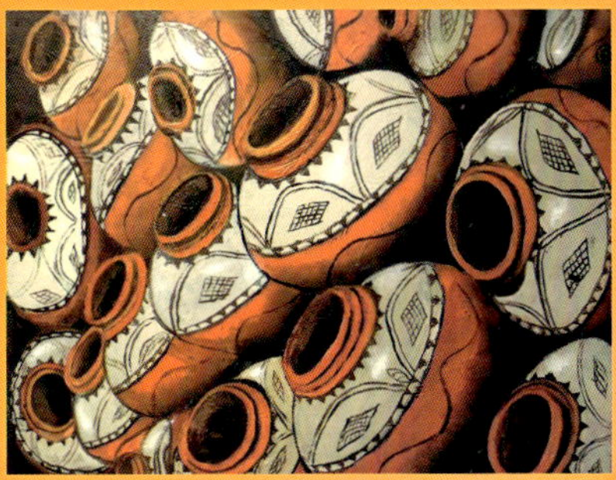

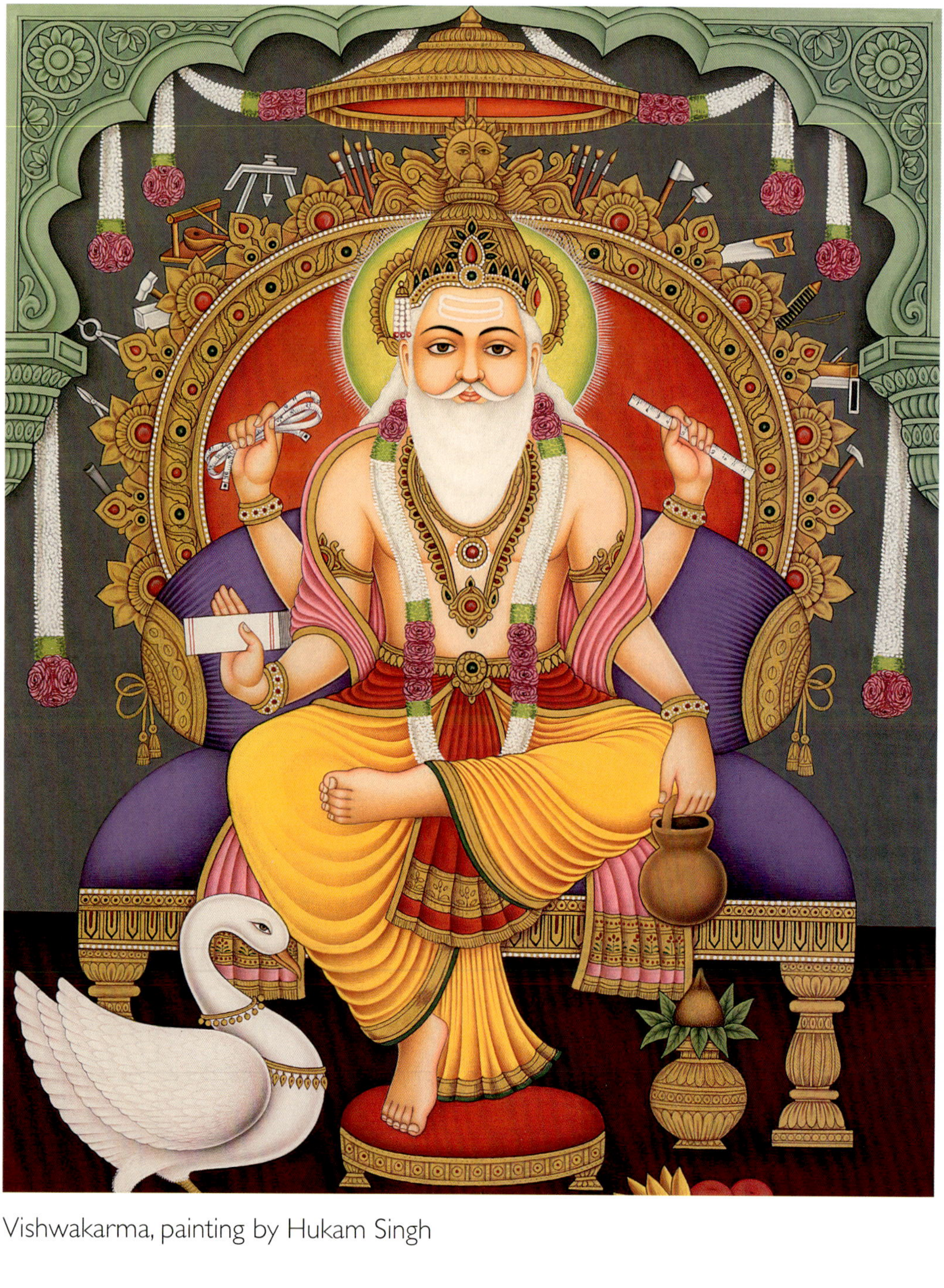

Vishwakarma, painting by Hukam Singh

It was a typical May morning in Delhi; hot and humid, the wind was still, the Gulmohar was ablaze with orange flowers, the sky was hazy and even the birds were less chirpy. Parrots sat silently on a branch and it seemed as if they had nothing to say to each other. From a distance the sounds of a morning *aarti* were heard. It was the beginning of Megha's summer holidays. Her mother had watered the tulsi plant in the garden and was making a simple rangoli at the threshold. Megha, still dressed in her night clothes, came and sat next to her mother, gave her a big hug and asked:

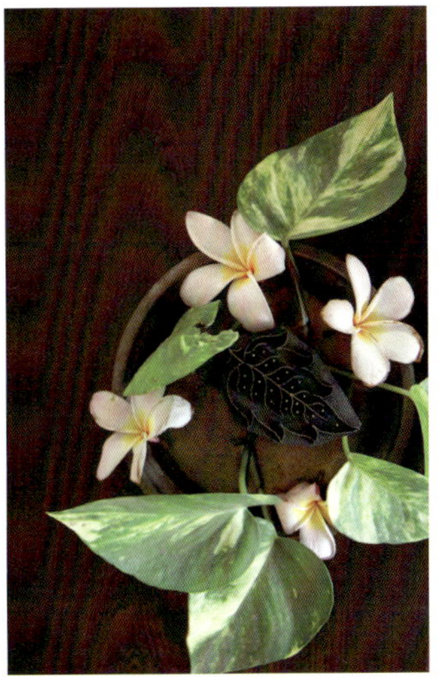

"Why are rangolis made at the threshold of the home?"
"Because," her mother said, "thresholds are at the border of the comfort and security of home and the chaos and uncertainty of the world outside. It is the intermediate space where Ganapati presides. It is a point of transition that we need to understand and celebrate."

Megha did not understand this totally but she took a little bit of the rangoli powder and made a few dots in the pattern on the floor.

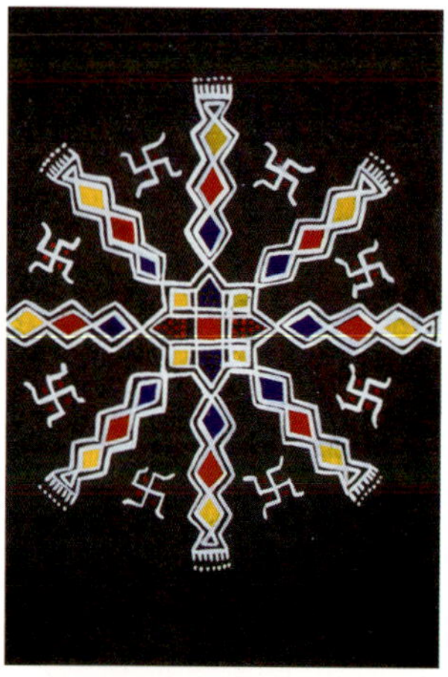

"Use red powder for that," her mother said. "A bindu should always be red like the sun, for it is very auspicious."
"Why is that?" Megha asked.
"Because a bindu is a mark of *purnatva*, fullness, of totality, of the coming together of matter and spirit."

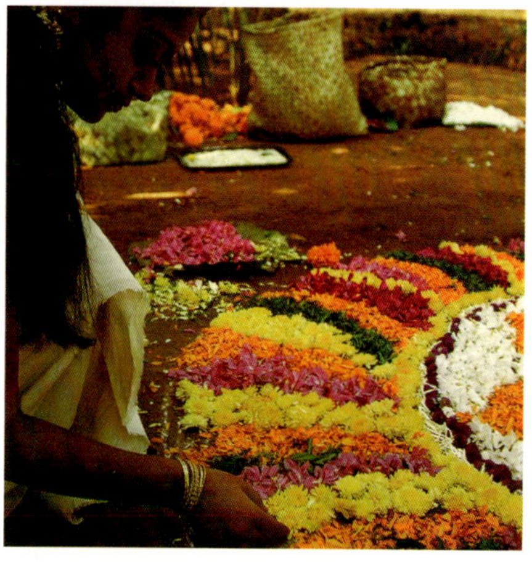

Her mother had finished making the rangoli and as she threw her *pallu* over her shoulder, she went into the garden and Megha followed her barefoot.
"Look at the carpet of Parijatak flowers!" she exclaimed and soon both of them were picking up the flowers and gathering them in a large leaf.
"The Parijatak is one of our five sacred trees and it was Krishna who brought it down to earth from heaven," her mother said.

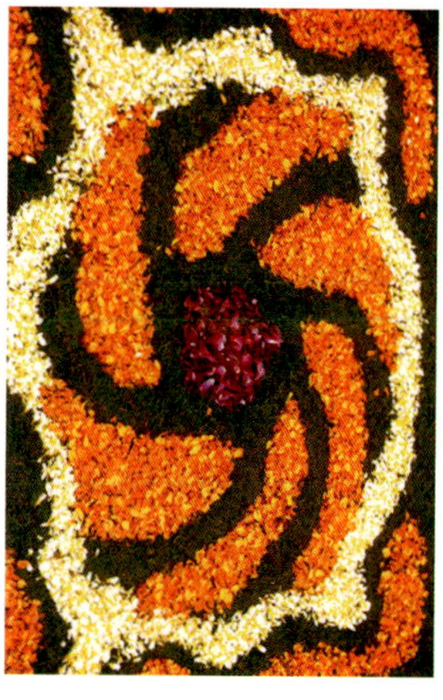

"Which are the other four?" Megha asked, always wanting to know more.
"They are Mandara, Harichandana, Kalpataru and Samtanaka," her mother replied.
Megha was now fully awake and was sitting inside with the Parijatak flowers on a table in front of her, making a mala.

"What a lovely mala you have made," her mother said as Megha handed it over to her.
"Let us put it around the image of Krishna in our shrine. Did you know that making flower garlands is one of our sixty-four arts?"

"What are the other sixty-three arts, and what is the difference between art and craft?" Megha asked, obviously interested in the question of arts and crafts. Her school teacher had given her a project on Origami for the summer and she was reading up on various crafts.

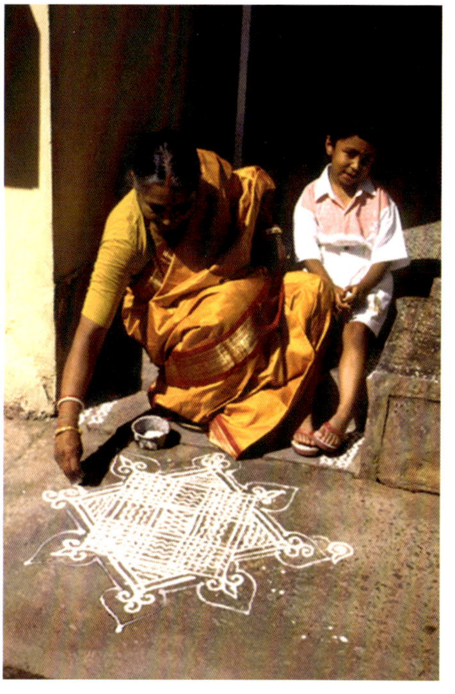

"Actually, the distinction between art and craft is a Western concept," her mother said adjusting her glasses. "There is no special word for art or craft in our Indian languages. Even the word kala, which is commonly used for art, really means *kruti* or the method. It was fashionable to call craft as a lower form of art but that is not true anymore."
"What should we call them then?" Megha was

now animated and wanted to know all about Indian crafts. Her mother sensed this and putting the newspaper down she looked at Megha and said, "I have an idea, a plan for today. I will postpone the errands that I had to run and instead, why not the two of us go to Dilli Haat? There you will be able to see a lot of crafts and craftsmen and women. You should enjoy it. Go and quickly get ready."

Megha ran upstairs and, after her bath, put on her new red kurta that her mother had bought for her. Her hair was done in two braids with a red ribbon and she put on some yellow bangles and a pair of dangling earrings. Megha liked to dress up and today was a special day as she was going to the craft fair. Soon they drove to Dilli Haat. A small crowd had already gathered outside and while her mother stood at the ticket counter Megha looked around and was very excited. The place was packed with different craftspeople who were setting up their shops. She could see woodwork and fabrics, paintings, and a person who had a lot of toys in a basket and was practising a tune on his small musical instrument. There were a few odd policemen and security personnel wandering around. Under a

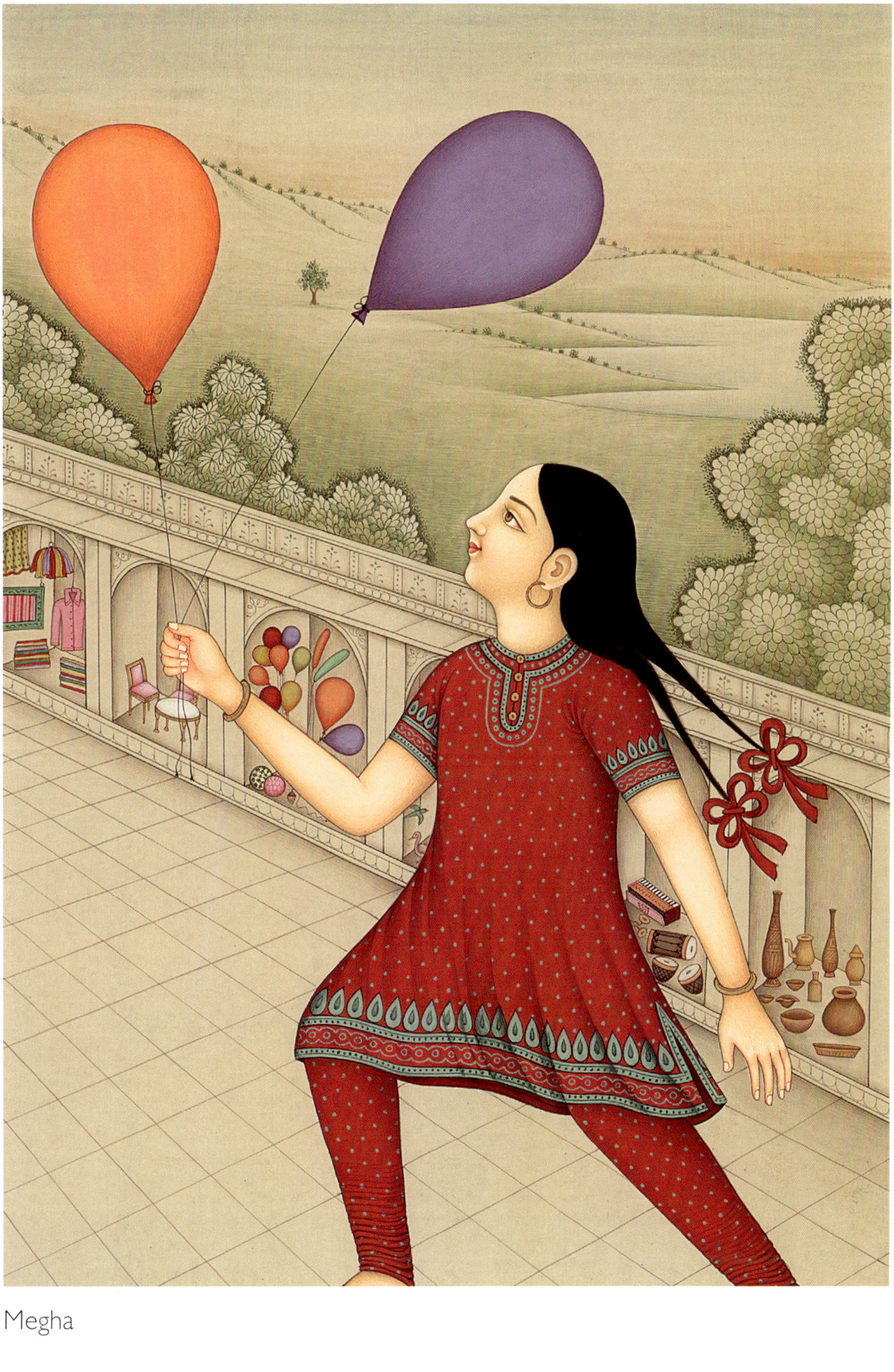

Megha

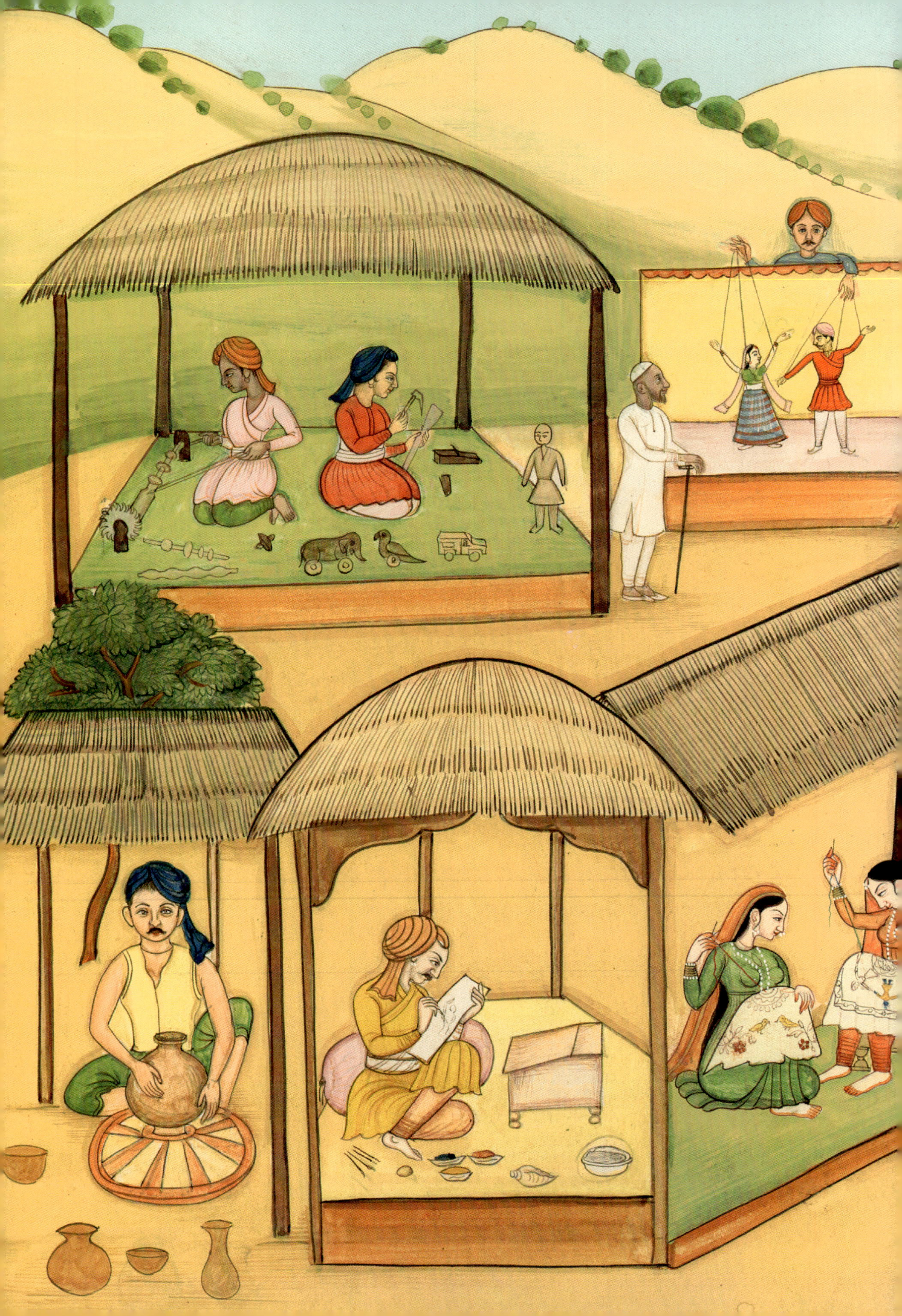

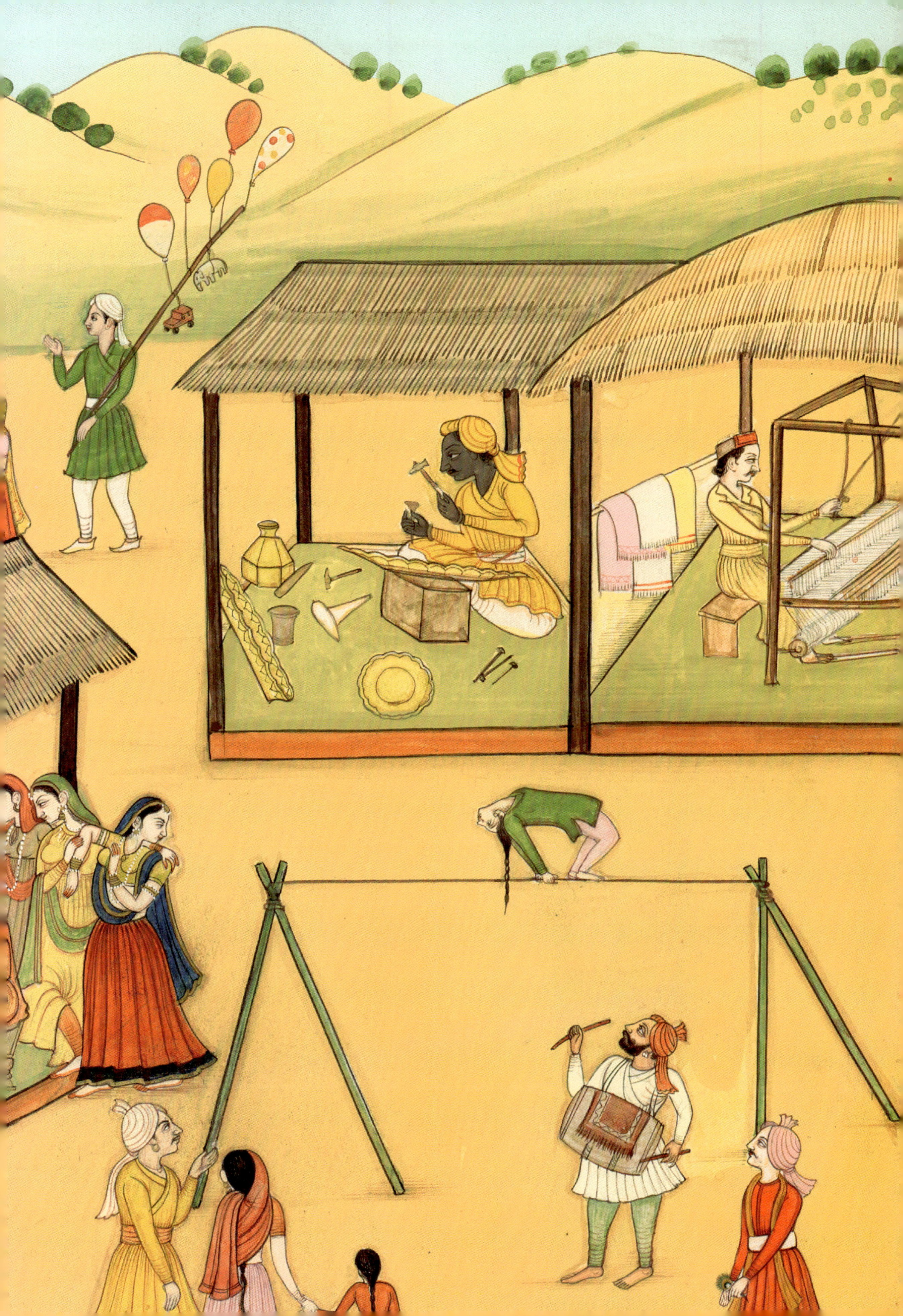

tree there was a monkey man but his monkeys were just sitting and observing everything. All of this had the appearance of a mela. Megha had been to some melas before but never to a craft mela and she was really excited. She decided that she would study all the crafts that there were to see and write about them in her assignment for school.

Just then her mother appeared with two tickets and they made their way into the Haat. It was still early and most of the stalls were just opening. Many were sweeping the area outside their own stalls and raising a cloud of dust. Others who had finished cleaning were spraying water on the earth to settle the dust. Some were lighting incense and some others were doing an impromptu *aarti* with a small diya and flowers in front of an image of Ganesha that they had installed on a makeshift shelf in their stall. Some others were hanging their wares on hooks under their canopies. Others were greeting each other over a cup of tea in a *kulhad.* A couple of elderly men were drawing on their huqqa. There was a different quality to the morning light at the Haat.

Megha was struck by the ambience of the Haat. Everyone here was involved with crafts and there was a certain pride and self-respect in their behaviour and demeanour. They handled their wares with so much joy and care, for after all they had made them themselves and with their own hands. There was a sense of happiness about them. Most of them were there as a family: father, mother, grandparents and even their children. Some mothers were feeding their younger children while the older ones helped set up their stall. The day was just beginning and there was both expectation and excitement on the faces of the people, which was very different from the atmosphere in a mall. At a mall there were many shops, with glitzy lights, mannequins that did not smile, a synthetic ambience, salespeople who were eager to sell you their product, but Megha wondered how much they knew about what they were selling. Did they have pride in their products? Did they know who had made them, whether it was handmade or made in a factory? At the Haat the atmosphere was that of a home and a family; they addressed her as "beti" or "baby", smiled at her, welcomed her and were eager to show their wares to her, whether or not she bought anything.

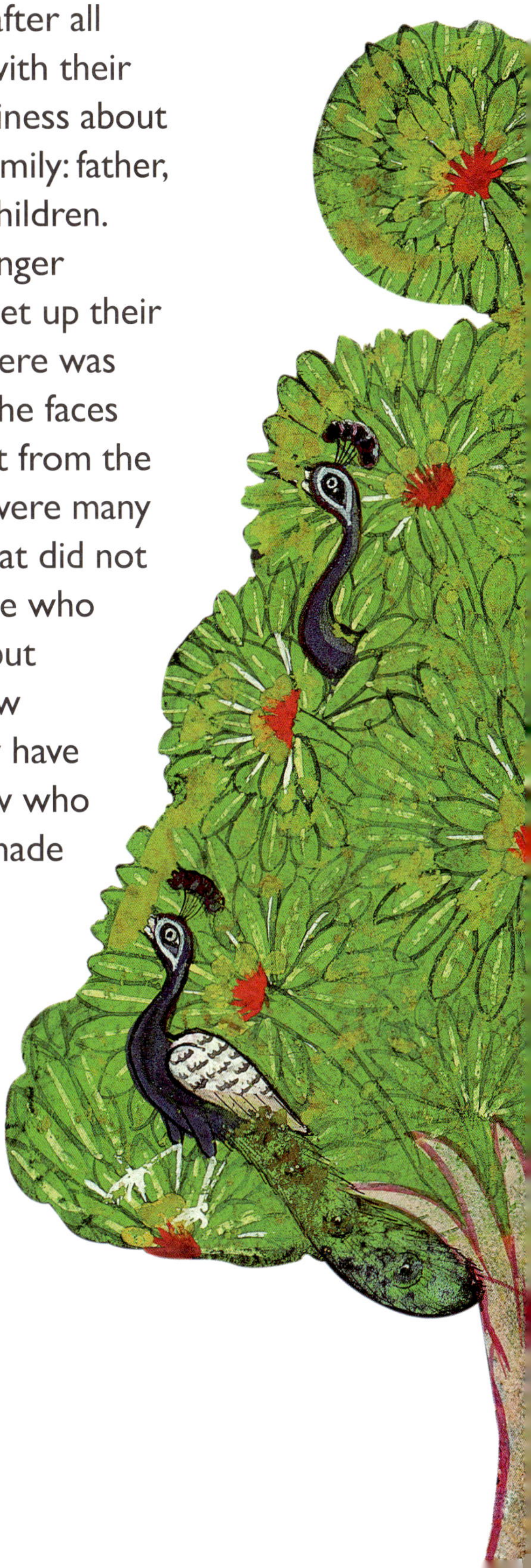

Megha felt attracted towards the various crafts but even more so to the people involved with them. She wanted to learn all about the crafts, meet the people, speak to them and become a part of their family. Just then her mother, who was looking at saris in a shop, came there and Megha asked, "Can we stay here all day? I want to talk to all the people and learn about their crafts and their life."

"I have only two hours to spare. Do what you want within that time. I must get home by lunchtime as I have a number of things to do," her mother said.

Megha was disappointed. She sat under a tree where a sadhu was also sitting. The sadhu asked her, "Beti, you look sad. What is the matter?"

"I want to spend the whole day here and learn all about the crafts and the people, their lives and lifestyles, the way they make their crafts and the various materials that they use. I want to

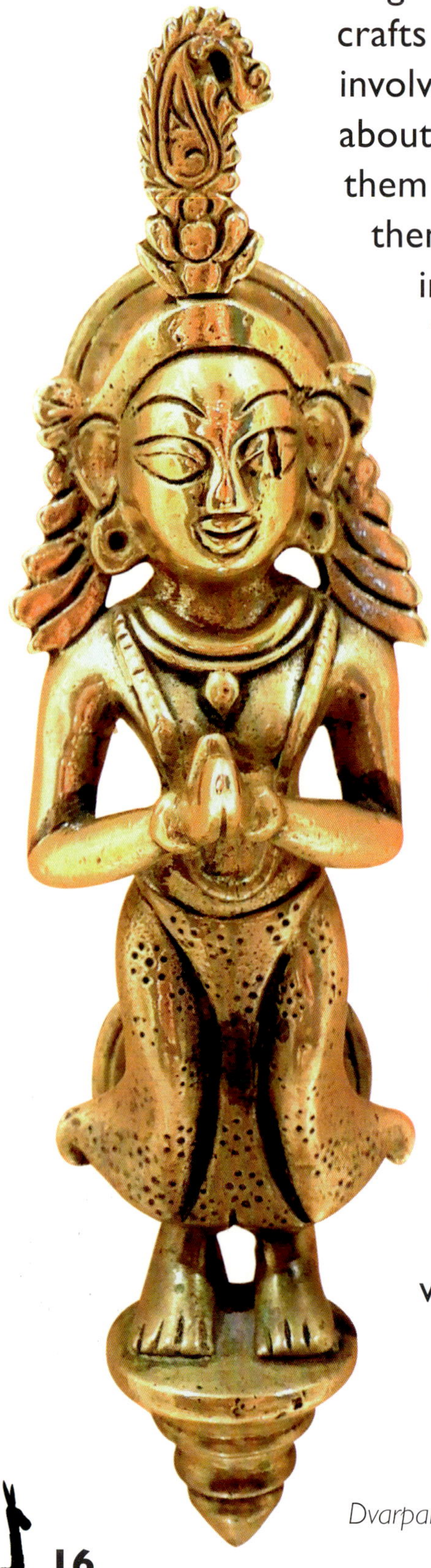

Dvarpala as a door knob

be a part of them but my mother said no." There was a look of disappointment written all over her face. The glow that she had worn when she entered the Haat had disappeared and instead her eyes were downcast. The sadhu looked at her with his soft and gentle eyes and said, "Do you really want to meet these craftspeople and learn about their skills? I can help you do that."

"How would you be able to do that?" Megha asked. She looked up to him and her eyes lit up.

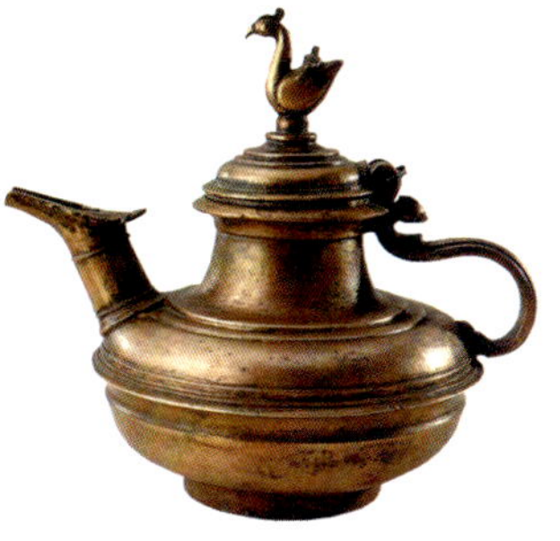

"I am not an ordinary sadhu but am Vishwakarma in disguise. I visit all craft fairs all over the country to be with my family of craftsmen. I am their presiding deity and I look after their welfare."

Megha could not believe what she was hearing. Was this real or was she dreaming? Her heart was racing and she tried to look at the sadhu but felt shy. She wondered whether to run to her mother or to stay with the sadhu. She had never heard of Vishwakarma. Was he a god or a rishi? She had never been to a temple of Vishwakarma. But there was something very reassuring about his looks, very comforting about his presence. She felt

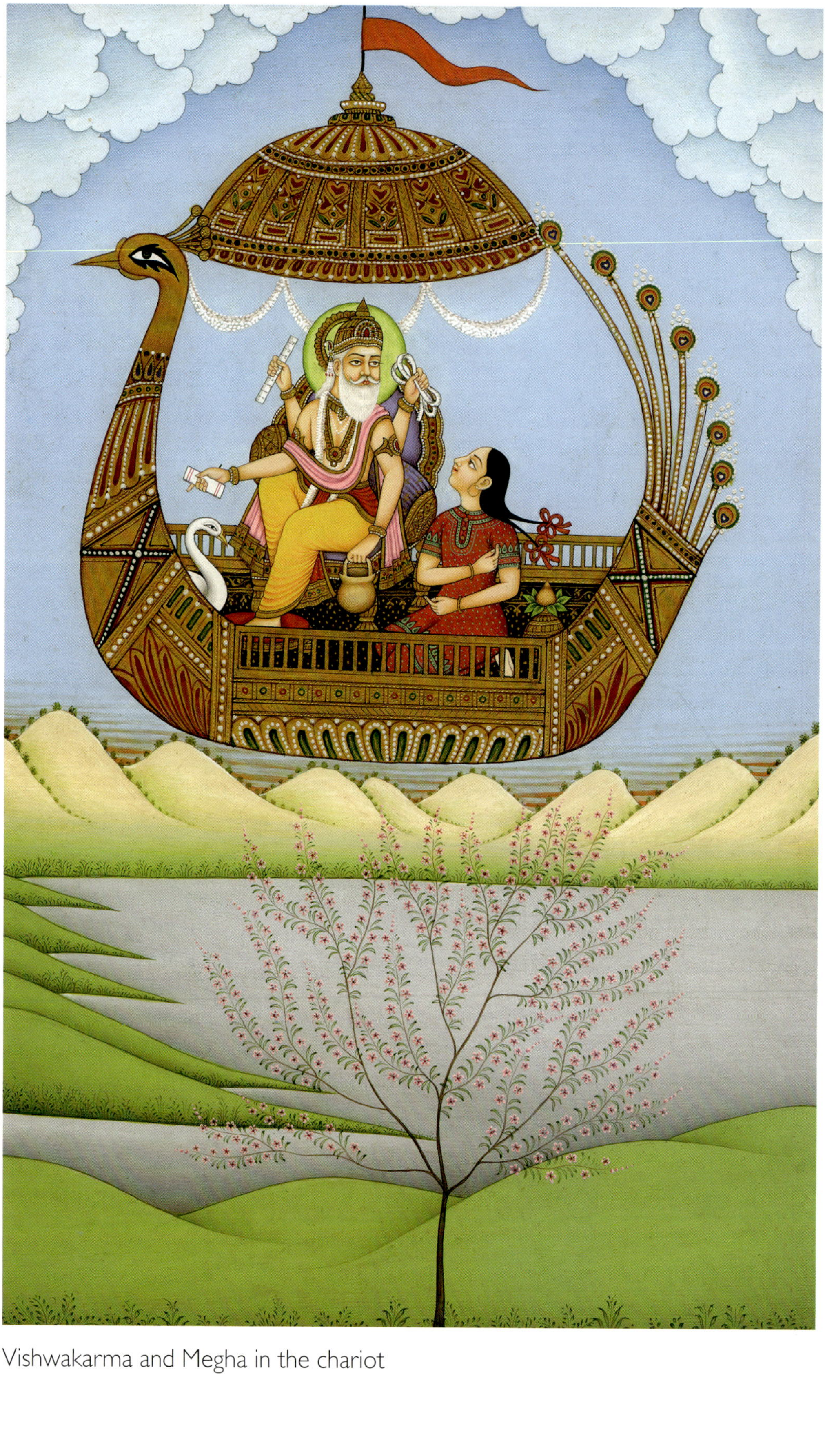

Vishwakarma and Megha in the chariot

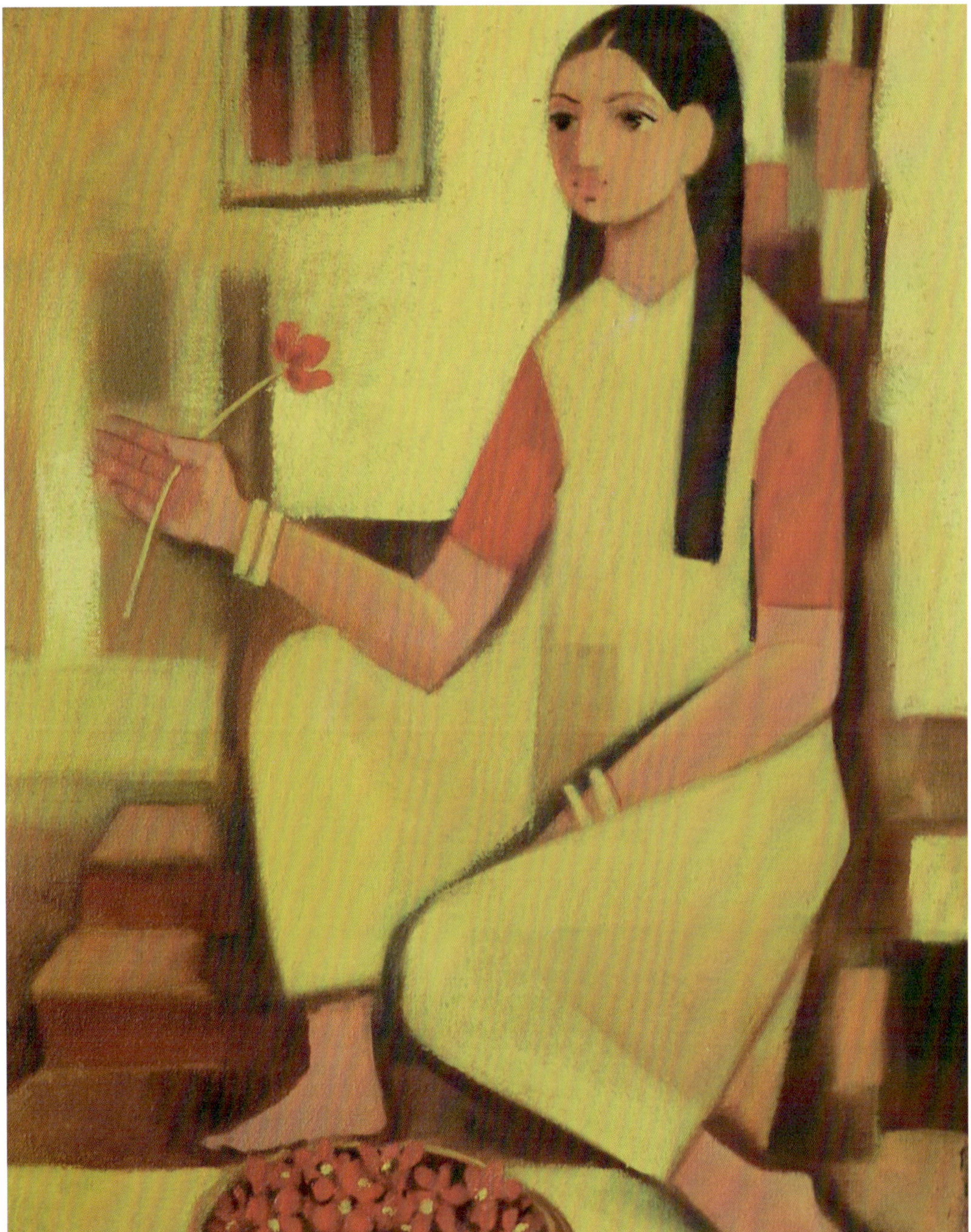

A flower seller at Dilli Haat, painting by Harish Raut

safe and protected around him.
"Where do you live?" Megha sat upright and picked up strength to talk to him.

"I live in heaven but I come down to earth from time to time. This time I have to come to visit all my children in Dilli Haat. Come with me and I will take you all over our country. You will be able to meet all *shilpis* and their families and see how they create all the beautiful crafts. We will be back in an hour."

Megha's face lit up. She was wonderstruck and excited. She looked around to find her mother but she was very far away talking to some friends.

"Will my mother be angry if I went with you?" she asked.
"She will not even know as we will be flying through the sky in a special celestial car."

Megha was bursting with excitement. She tied her chunni as she prepared to go with Vishwakarma in the *udankhatola*. This was a dream come true for her. She would fly all over India and meet so many craftsmen in their own homes. As she stepped into the celestial car her heart was racing but there was a glow on her face. Vishwakarma came and sat next to her and with a wave of his hand made the car fly into the sky and very soon they were up in the clouds. Megha felt like she was in heaven and recalled the time when she had climbed a magic tree and met so many heavenly beings. This time it was different as Vishwakarma was beside her. Pointing to the vast sky all around he said, "This is my home, this is where I live and it's from this place in the sky that I keep a watch over all my children." As the chariot was speeding through the sky Megha's chunni fluttered and as she looked outside she saw little huts and villages, fields and farms. How different things looked when one was up in the air. Holding her hand, Vishwakarma said, "How beautiful is our country, majestic our mountains, sacred our rivers and blessed our earth. And it is on this earth that we live, in it are the footfalls of our rishis who mediated to find the meaning of life, it is in the earth that we till and plant our seeds, it is from the earth that trees rise and grow to reach the sky, under this earth are the secret springs of water which sustain us, it is from the rhythms of the earth that different seasons

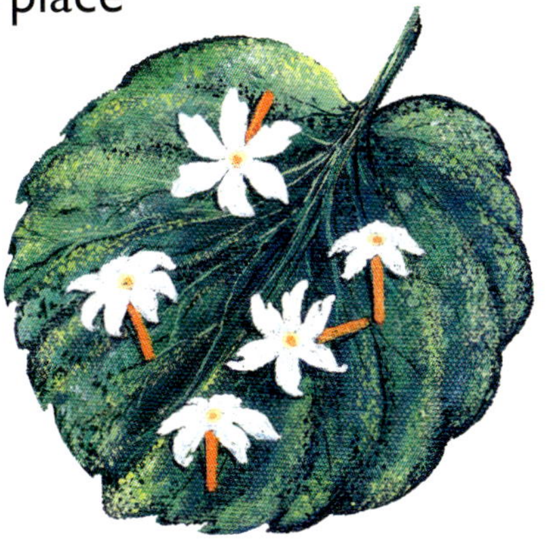

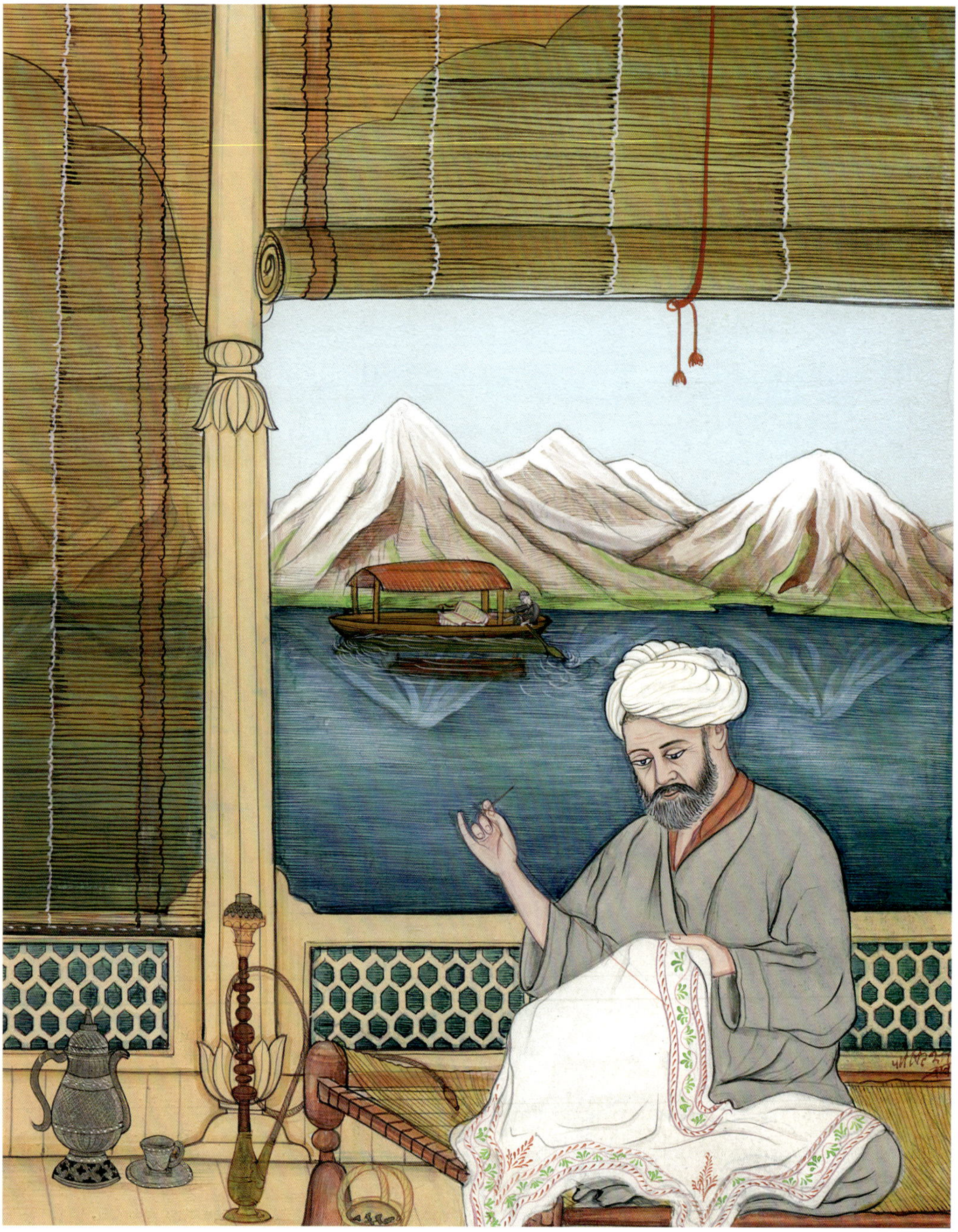

A Kashmir shawl embroiderer, painting by Parikshit Sharma

arise and it is from a handful of earth that our potters make our pots." And as Vishwakarma was describing the beauty of the earth he chanted the Prithvi Sukta to Megha.

Megha did not understand the hymn that Vishwakarma chanted but she loved the sound and felt a closeness to the earth. Just then Vishwakarma said, "Get ready for our first stop. We will touch down in Kashmir," and with those words he made the chariot descend to earth.

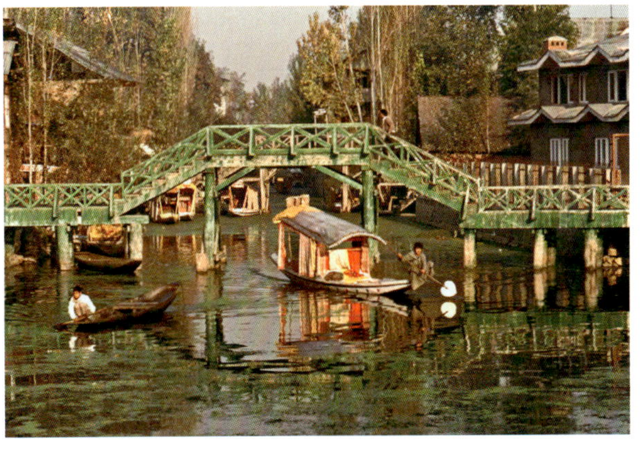

Megha found herself on the shores of the Jhelum river and they went inside a houseboat where an elderly man was working on a fabric. Seeing Vishwakarma the man got up and offered salutations and Megha in turn said namaste to him.

"Meet Kumar Raina. He is an embroiderer and he works on shawls." Raina beckoned Megha to come and sit next to him. He was sitting on a pillow on the ground and was drawing on his huqqa. Next to him was a *kangri* which kept him warm and a *samovar* which had saffron tea. "Making shawls is an ancient profession for us in Kashmir. On our mountains we have sheep and goats and we harvest their hair, which is spun into threads and then woven into a woolen fabric. This has been our family business since the time of the Mughals."

He pointed to a framed picture on the wall. "This is a portrait of Mughal emperor Jehangir. He was very fond of Kashmir shawls and called them *param naram*. He would have his *jamas* made from these shawls."
"Feel this." So saying he gave Megha a couple of shawls. "This is shatush and the other is pashmina. Feel how soft they are. You can fold them and pass them through a ring."

Megha felt both the shawls and even draped one over her shoulder. "Jehangir was very fond of flowers and would have us embroider flowers on the shawls. In his studio were accomplished artists who could paint every type of flower that grew in the Kashmir valley. Our forefathers would go to Agra to see these painted flowers and we would then reproduce them in our shawls."
Megha was spellbound by all this.
"Look at this," Raina said. "I am embroidering an *aam butta* or a mango pattern. This pattern

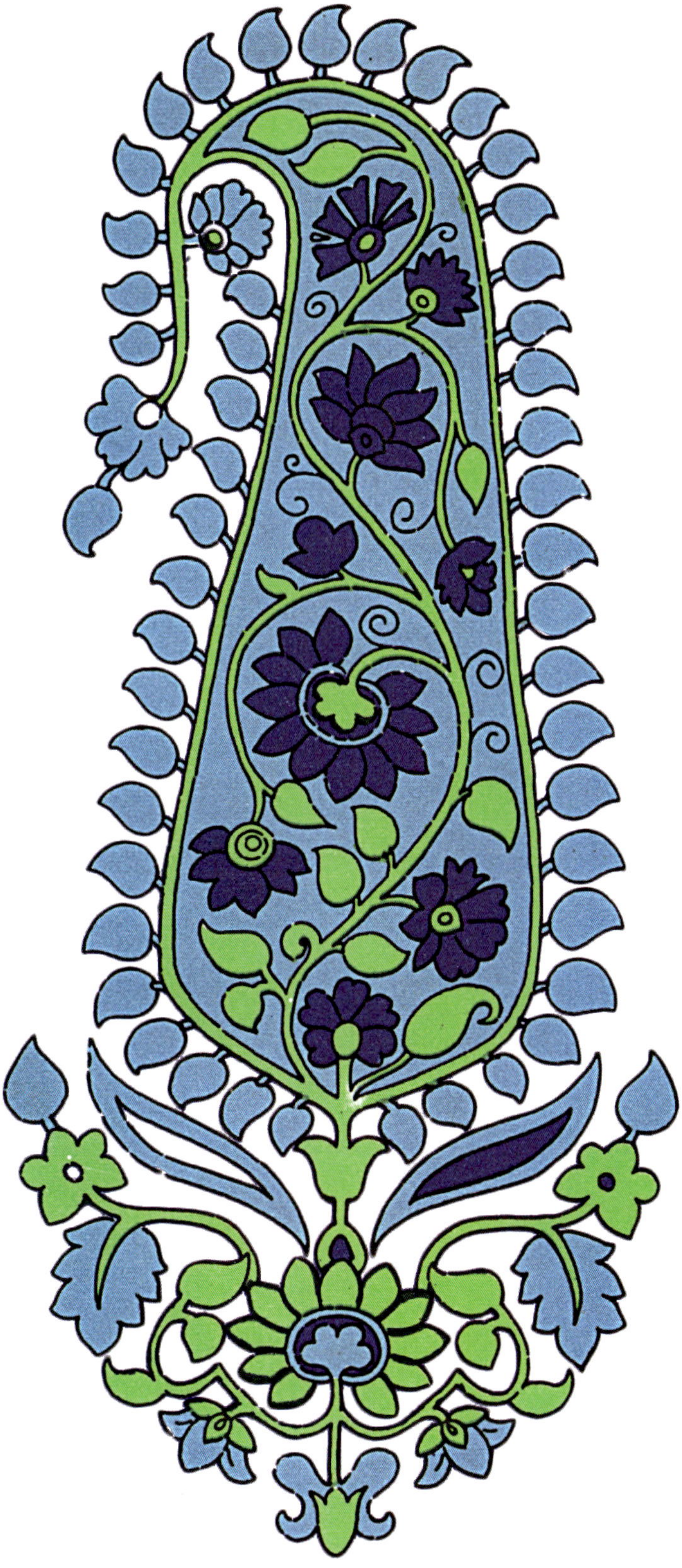

Aam butta, mango motif

came to India originally from Persia where it was meant to be a stylised cypress of a Saru tree. We in Kashmir modified it to look like a mango and Jehangir liked it so much that he wanted it on his *patkas* and *jamas*. From then it spread all over the country and today it is hard to find a fabric without the mango motif!"

Raina took a piece of cloth that was lying around and quickly embroidered a mango pattern for Megha. Megha took this and thanked Raina.

"Be sure to come back and visit us again."

Vishwakarma held Megha's hand and they returned to the chariot, which was soon in the air.
"Can we go to Agra to see where Jehangir lived?"
Vishwakarma smiled. "He does not live there any more but we can go and meet some marble workers. They too are children. They create copies of the Taj Mahal and other objects in marble."
Vishwakarma landed his chariot in the outskirts of Agra. There were a row of shops where craftsmen were working on marble.

"Come, let us meet Sukhvinder who makes boxes out of marble."

Megha and Vishwakarma went to Sukhvinder's shop. There were pieces of marble lying around and Sukhvinder was working on them with a small chisel. Seeing Vishwakarma he got up, asked them to come in and made them sit on low chairs in his shop.

"What is your name, beti?" he asked.

"I am Megha and I want to know more about the marble work that you are doing."

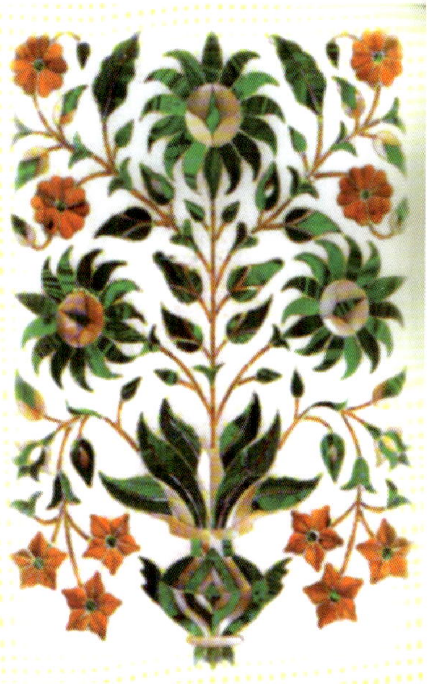

"I'll get to that but first, let me tell you a story. The year was 1607 and in the dusty streets of Agra a meena bazaar was held. It was a day of fun and frolic when boys and girls, men and women mingled. Women removed their veils and exchanged glances with men while shopkeepers showed off their wares. There were silk and glass beads, perfume and jewellery. The ambience was festive, mood of the people was joyous and there was excitement in the air. At one shop a vivacious and charismatic fifteen-year-old girl, just like you, was in charge and was in animated conversations with her customers. A handsome sixteen-year-old boy bursting with energy stopped by her store and mischievously asked the price of a piece of glass that was glittering in the sunlight. The girl, with a twinkle in her eye, said that it was no glass but was actually a diamond and that the young man should buy it, whereupon the boy slipped 10,000 rupees into her hand and ran away with the piece of glass. This was the dawn of a romance that made its presence felt not just all over India but the world over; a romance that has been unmatched in its tender beauty and the legacy that it has left behind. For that sweet fifteen-year-old was none other than Arjumand, the daughter of Asaf Khan, prime minister of Jehangir, and the sixteen-year-old boy was Prince Khurram, son of Jehangir. Khurram went on to become Shah Jahan and Arjumand became Mumtaz Mahal, and even today as we walk through Taj Mahal we hear the sweet whispers of their love. We are descendants of the people who made Taj Mahal."

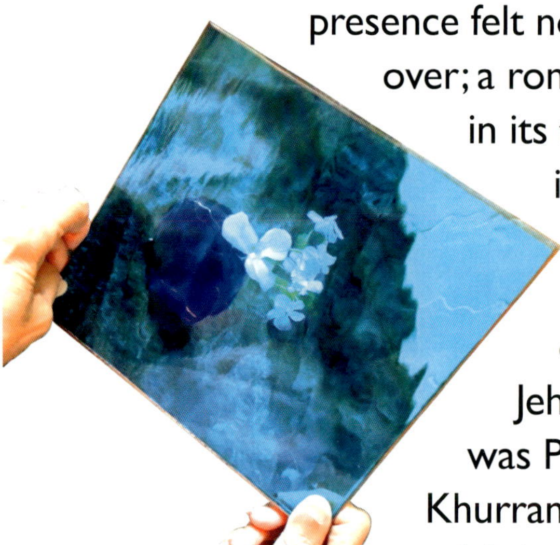

Megha was spellbound by this tale of romance and had a distant look in her eyes, as if wondering whether she would become like Mumtaz Mahal.

Interrupting her silence Sukhvinder said, "Come now and touch this marble. Hold it against the light and see how translucent it is, and so soft to the touch. The makers of the Taj were not only experts in working with marble but also knew how to place precious stones in them. Did you know that the Taj had about twenty different varieties of precious stones embedded in the marble?"

Vishwakarma steered his chariot towards Varanasi and as they flew over the Ganga, Megha saw many people taking a dip in its sacred waters.

"Varanasi is home to many saints and rishis. Tulsidas composed *Ramcharitmanas* on the banks of Ganga and Kabir would sing and weave here. Even Buddha preached his first sermon here. Let us go and visit the Kabir Math. Kabir was a weaver and he would sing his bhajans as he sat on his loom."

"Tell me more about weaving," Megha said as the chariot landed in the Math.

Vishwakarma sat under a pipal tree and spoke. "Weaving is an ancient tradition of India and weaving and philosophy share many common words—words such as sutra and tantra. It was in the growing, spinning, weaving, dyeing, printing and embroidering of cotton that the Indian craftspeople found their richest expression. Threads or sutra are an important part of Indian traditions, both religious and secular. There is a sense of wonder in creating thread from a cotton pod and then weaving it into fabric.

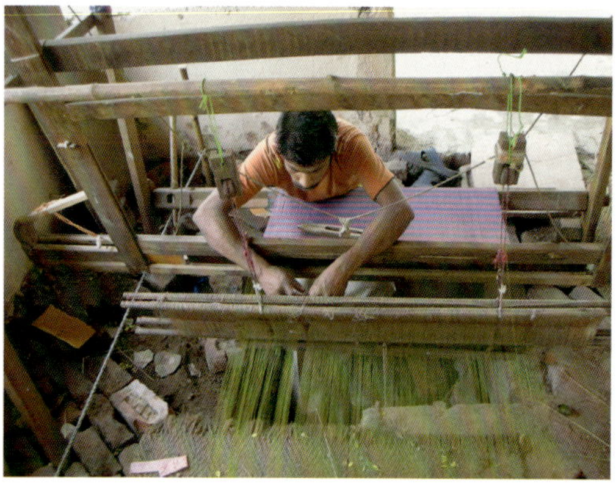

"Wrapping a thread around the trunk of a tree is done for the granting of a wish. In certain tribal villages a continuous thread is tied around the periphery of the village and this is believed to contain the good and ward off evil. Coloured threads serve as *vastra* for the deity in a puja and the devotee ends the puja by tying a thread on his wrist. Some of the deepest sentiments, such as between a sister and brother, are expressed by tying a thread, as in a rakhi. And it is from threads that fabrics of all kinds are woven.

"Weaving has often been compared to music—both are fine arts and done with dedication and *latifa* or pleasure. To fully understand a certain piece of textile, its colour and texture, design

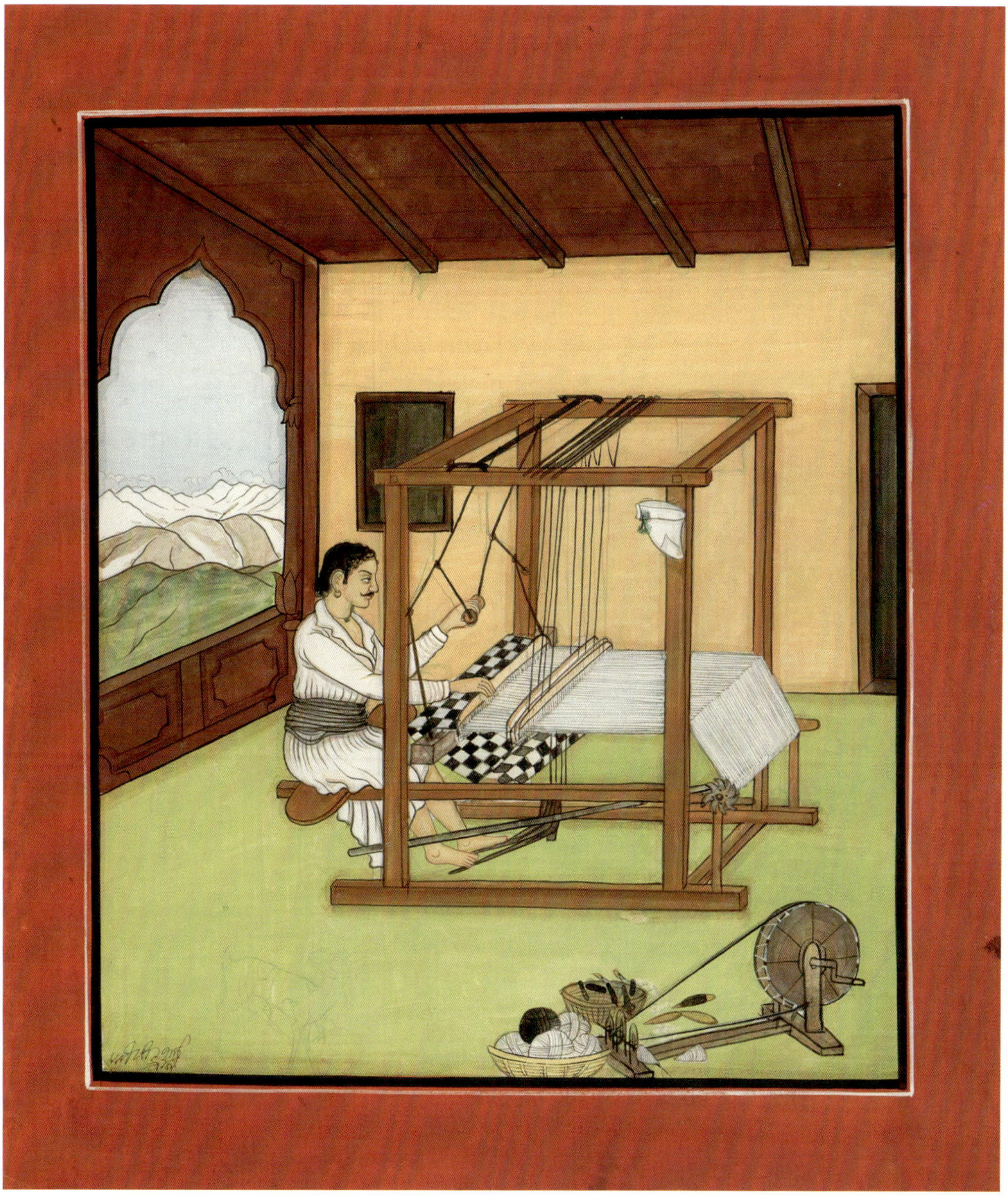

A weaver, painting by Parikshit Sharma

and motifs, one must bring to it not only one's sight but touch as well. Just as music begins with a single note, textile begins with a single thread. Also, like the many notes of the musical scale, there are many types of threads and they can be combined in multiple ways to produce a fabric. The loom is the weaver's instrument and he adjusts and sets it like a musician tunes his instrument. When the weaver fills his *bani* or weft and throws his shuttle, it is as if the musician has started the alap, and like a raga, weaving has a certain rhythm or *laya*. Furthermore, just as a raga has a certain rasa or *rang*, the weaver infuses a certain feeling in what he weaves, and each fabric like each raga requires a different technique. The environment in which the weaver lives fills him with wonder; green leaves, the bark of a tree, roots of a date palm, fruits like the mango, birds and blossoms, the feather of a peacock, and the fine thread of a spiderweb fill him with delight and he incorporates that in

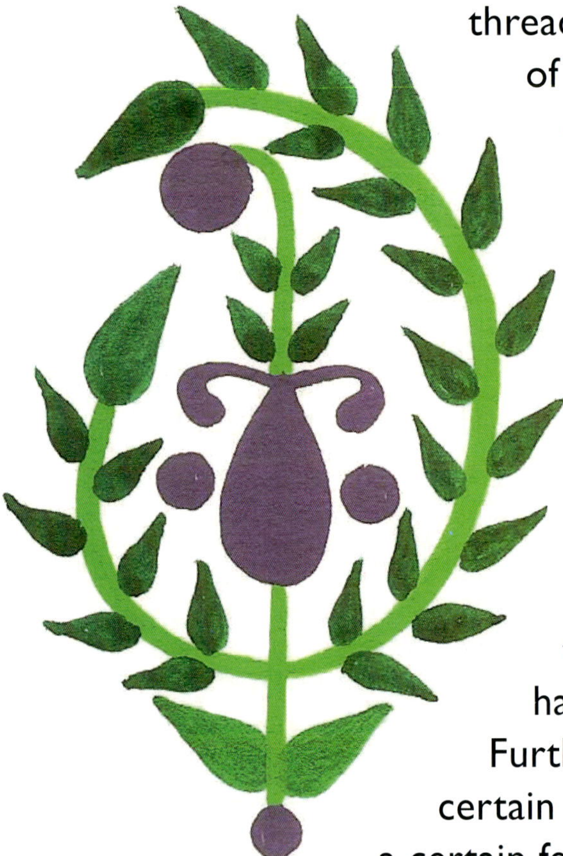

his fabric. And then there are colours which the weaver derives from the world around. Truly has it been said that weaving is like music."

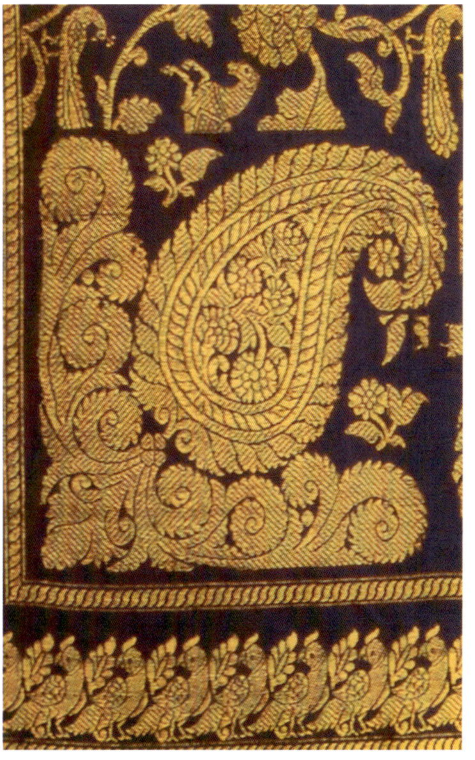

Megha heard this with great interest and realised the importance of weaving as a craft. She went around Kabir Math and decided that she was going to get a book of his *dohas*. Just then she saw an old man who was sitting on a wooden stool, chanting and counting beads.

"Will you please recite one of Kabir's *dohas* for me?" she asked.
"Of course I will. I know quite a few but this is my favourite.

Mati kahe kumhar se, tu kya rondhe mohe
Ek din aisa ayega, main rondhungi tohe"
(Says earth to the potter, you can't knead me forever.
A day shall come when I shall knead you)

Megha touched his feet and he in turn gave her a flower. She put this flower in her hair and went back to Vishwakarma who was already sitting in the chariot.

"Did you know that the wearing of a fabric appropriately was considered one of the sixty-four arts? A prerequisite in the wearing of a fabric was discernment of fabrics, or *pehchan*. *Pehchan* was the direct encounter with the fabric, its count, weight and feel, its modulation of colour, lustre and sheen. It implied a sense of proportion and of purpose, the ability to visualise the fabric lavished, draped and accented. The master weavers of beautiful fabrics were considered artists in their own right and claimed descent from me. As in traditional dance where every movement and gesture reflects the concept of a myth or belief, every woven and printed pattern, indeed every colour and form has a symbolic and distinct meaning, understood intuitively. Ornamentation in textiles is intrinsic to symbolic characterisation and never an erratic flourish. The decorative impulse towards a leaf, flower, fruit, creeper, bird or animal expresses not only the weaver's joy and freedom of creation but equally, the integration of human life with its surroundings."

Vishwakarma's chariot was now flying over Bihar. Megha showed no signs of fatigue or boredom. Rather, she wanted to soak in everything that she saw.

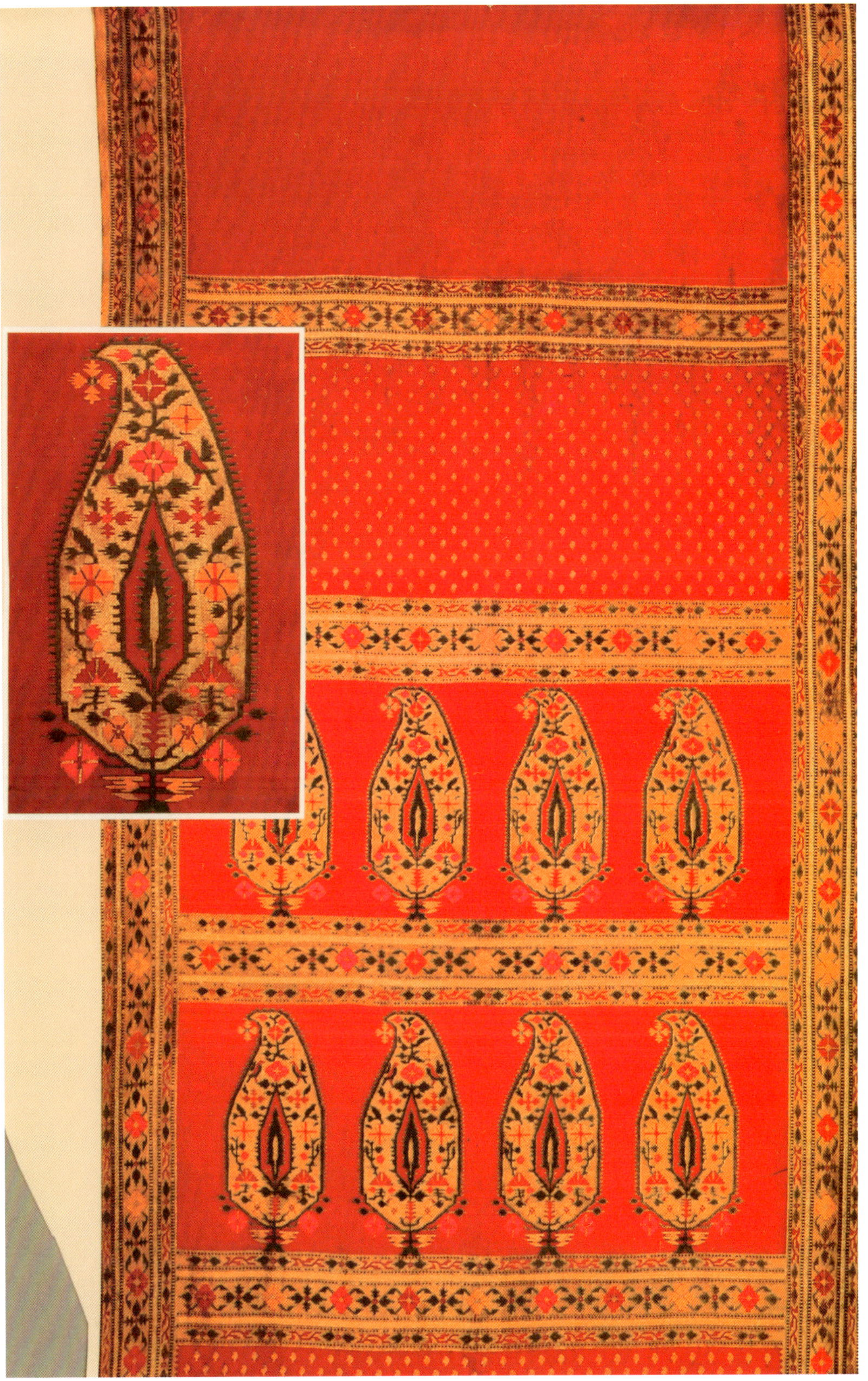

A brocade sari from Varanasi

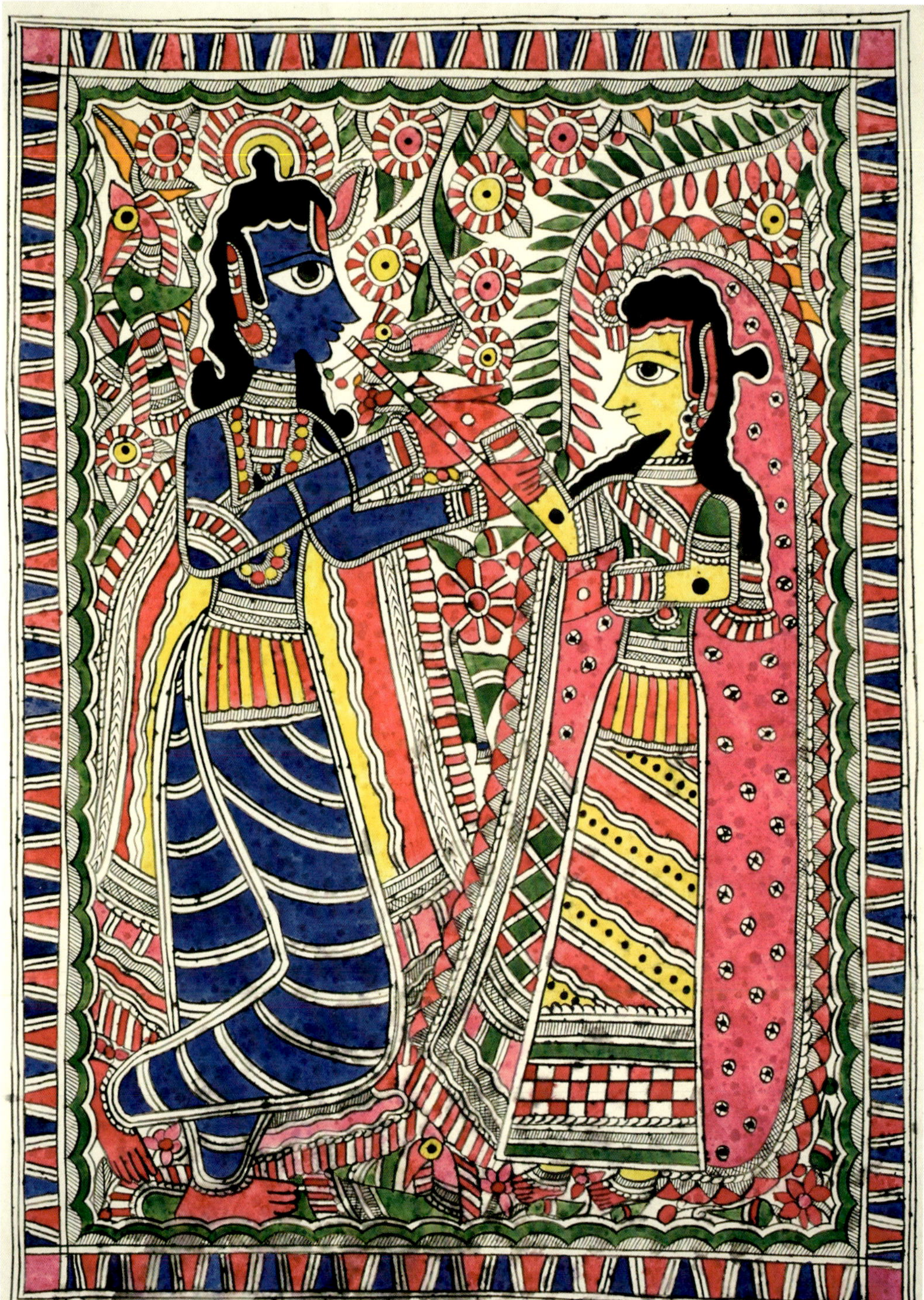

Madhubani painting

Vishwakarma spoke, "Bihar used to be called Mithila and it was here that both Buddha and Mahavira had walked. Did you know that the life of a village is sustained by social gatherings, festivals, rituals and processions, dancing and storytelling, births and marriages? One such village is Madhuban in the ancient kingdom of Mithila (in present-day northern Bihar), where a unique tradition of painting has been preserved by the women. The inspiration of these women's paintings is primarily religious and mythic. A variety of beliefs and ideas, stories and songs have been assimilated and have continued to exist since times ancient, and find expression in their visual representations. Done on mud walls with natural colours these murals are like a storybook, a visual education from which the community learns ancient epics and derives its values, assuages its fears and enrich their lives. These murals of Madhuban are a product of the communal spiritual experience and embody millennia of traditional knowledge. Passed down from mother to daughter, they ensure the living presence of our gods and goddesses."

Megha wanted to know more.

"One traditional Madhubani art form is the kohbar. The kohbar is a girl's proposal of marriage to a young man. Its basic design and composition is heavily charged with tantric erotic symbolism and features the bamboo and the lotus along with fishes and parrots, the *kalasha* and trees, and often shows a girl in a palanquin being taken to her in-laws' home. In colouring her blue the Madhubani women recall the love between Krishna and the *gopis* to their minds. The first kohbars in a courtship are used to wrap gifts like cosmetics, spices, jewellery and clothes. Later on they could be done on paper or baskets. And finally, during the days before the wedding, one of the walls of the marriage chamber is decorated with a large kohbar. The art of Madhuban finds its best expression in the kohbar ghar—the nuptial chamber where the newly married couple spend their first few days. Here, images of fertility and fecundity such as the lotus and the bamboo, the parrot and the fish share the same space as that of Radha and Krishna under the kadamba tree. Women of Madhuban eschew realism and

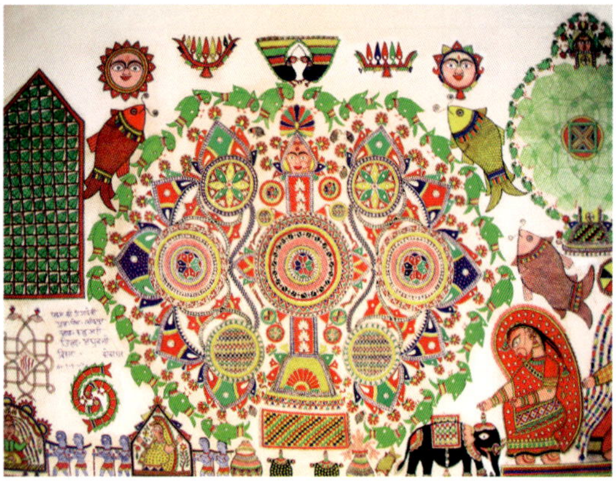

lyricism for the bold and the beautiful, with evocative colours and striking lines, to create a living space where the parrot is as important as the *gopi*. The flute of Krishna beckons and is heard along with the hooves of cows, for this is their interpretation of Vrindavana and it is entwined with their lives. Sexuality is represented in the kohbar as the root of all creation, and fertility and fecundity for these rustic Mithila women are the bases of spirituality. Life for the Mithila women is an organic whole and this finds expression in the kohbar."

Vishwakarma made the chariot descend in a field and a number of children came running towards it. They came near Megha and she in turn held their hands. The children took Megha, Vishwakarma in tow, with them to the village and showed them paintings that had been left to dry. In one home Sita Devi, an elderly lady who had no teeth and wore glasses, welcomed Megha whilst doing a painting of Radha-Krishna.

Sita Devi spoke, "Even when Madhubani art is created on paper rather than on walls, as it is these days, it retains its erudite imagery through the expressive eyes of Krishna and

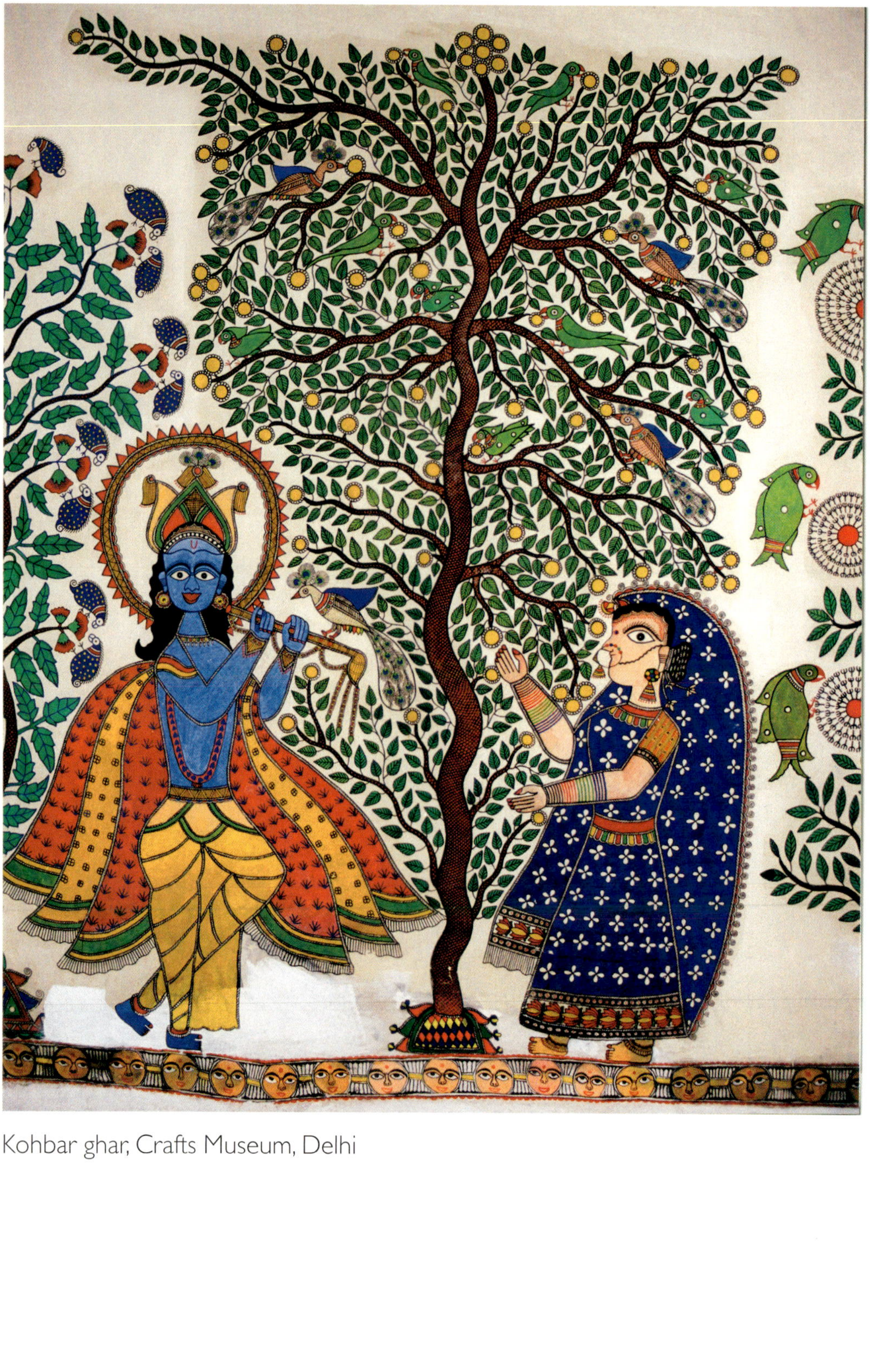

Kohbar ghar, Crafts Museum, Delhi

the expectant looks of the *gopis*. It is as if the words and songs of the Mithila poet Vidyapati are heard in these rustic but evocative paintings of Madhuban, and the women of Madhuban express their latent and often suppressed romantic feelings through them."

Ganga Devi from the house next door had come and she pitched in, "Another ritual painting in Madhuban is the aripan or the floor diagram, done with the same bright colours. It incorporates tantric motifs and depictions of deities and is a part of every ritual and ceremony. The women of Mithila believe that if an aripan is properly done the deity will come and reside in it and bless their household. The world of gods and goddesses is never far from our day-to-day world of commerce and daily existence, and this makes such creations not merely art but objects of beauty."

Megha wandered in and out of many houses and the women of Madhuban urged her to stay with them for a whole day, even offering to teach her how to paint. Megha looked expectantly at Vishwakarma who said that they still have a lot of travelling to do but that next year he would bring her back and let her stay with these women artists. Megha reluctantly took their leave but not before Ganga Devi had applied a tilak of kumkum to her with the words of blessing, "*Sada sukhi raho.*"

Megha and Vishwakarma took their leave and as they were flying over northern Bihar he pointed to the town of Darbhanga and said:

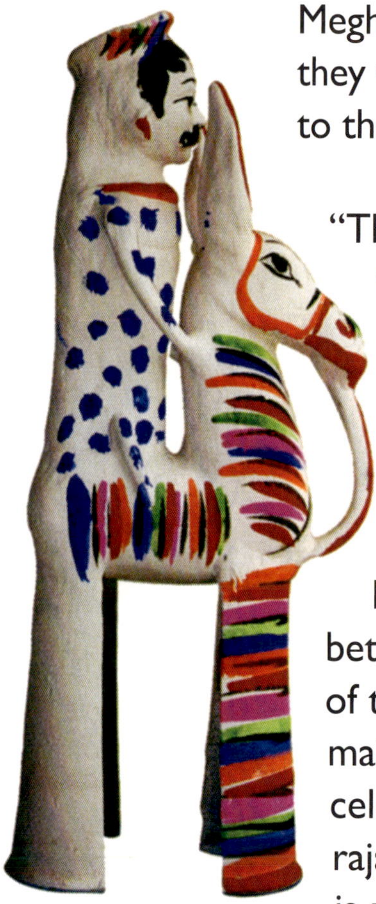

Terracotta horse from Darbhanga, Bihar

"The kumbhars or potters of Darbhanga are famous for making colourful terracota horses with riders. Legend has it that Raja Shailesh was a local hero of the community of potters who ruled in the fifth century. He was a powerful king and his kingdom spanned across Tibet, Bhutan, Nepal and Mithila. There were constant struggles between the dominant and the subaltern castes of this community and Shailesh was able to maintain peace between them. The potters celebrate him with terracotta images of this raja. The image is painted in vibrant colours and is particularly popular in Bihar."

From Madhuban, Vishwakarma steered his chariot east towards Bengal and in no time

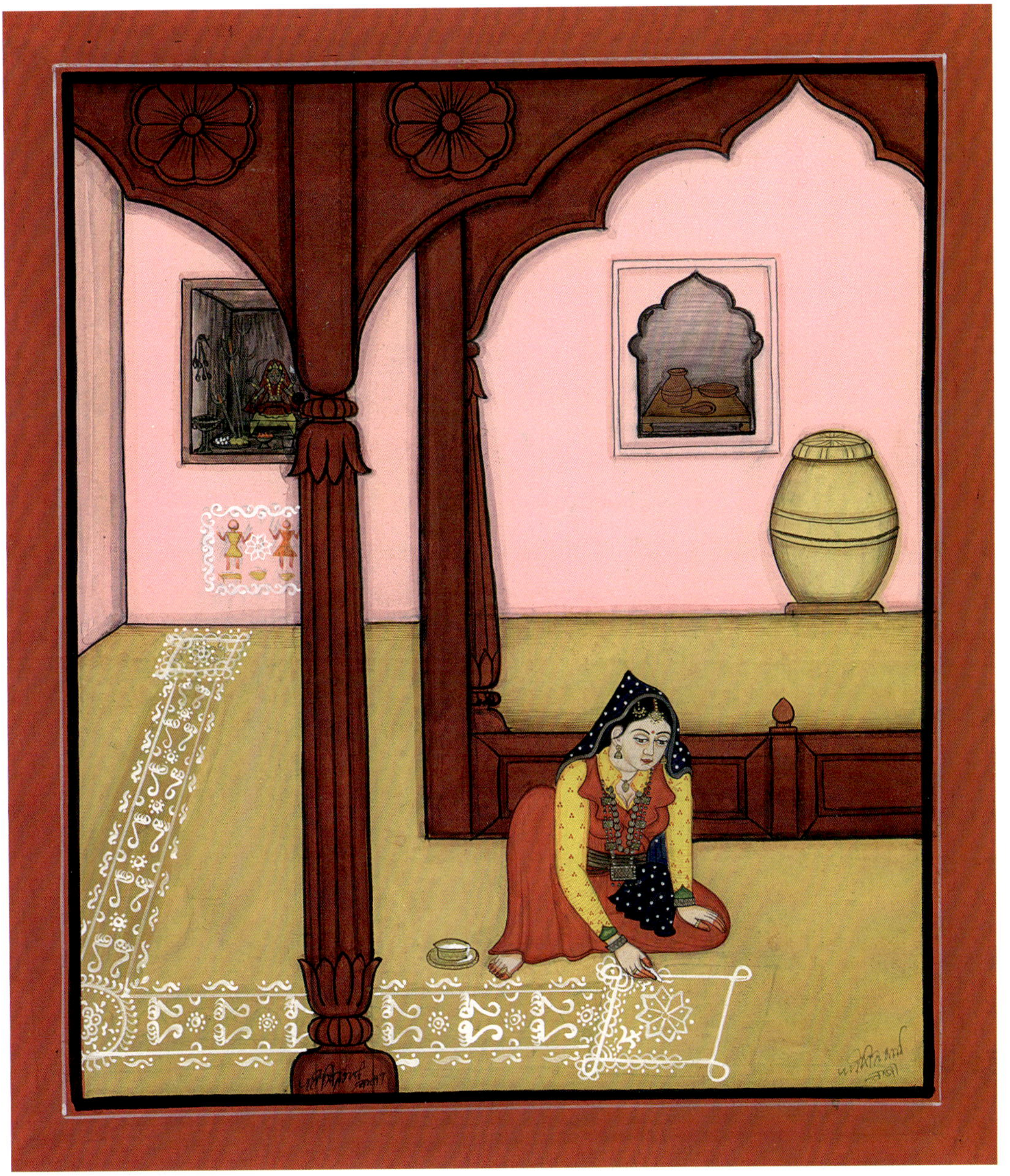

Rangoli in a home in Madhuban

they were flying over the Kali temple in Kolkata. Megha looked down.

If the paintings of Madhuban bring to life the rustic presence of Krishna, those of Kalighat are reminiscent of the *patas* of Bengal. Tracing their lineage to the *patuas* or *pata* painters and eventually to Vishwakarma, nineteenth century saw the emergence of painters who were displaced from the courts. These painters settled themselves in the vicinity of Kalighat temple and produced iconic images in a characteristic style, mainly for pilgrims. Featuring robust colours and bold lines, with iconic figures against a blank background, the Kalighat figures had an aura of simplicity and modernity about them. While painting mythic figures, including Krishna, the Kalighat painters also expressed themselves through satirical images of the bhadralok of Bengal, the dandy and the babu, as well as the prevalent scandals like the Elokeshi episode. It is in this context that the Kalighat paintings of Krishna must be understood. Nineteenth-century Calcutta was at the vanguard of modernity, with both nationalism and artistic renaissance stirring the people into action, and it is out of these

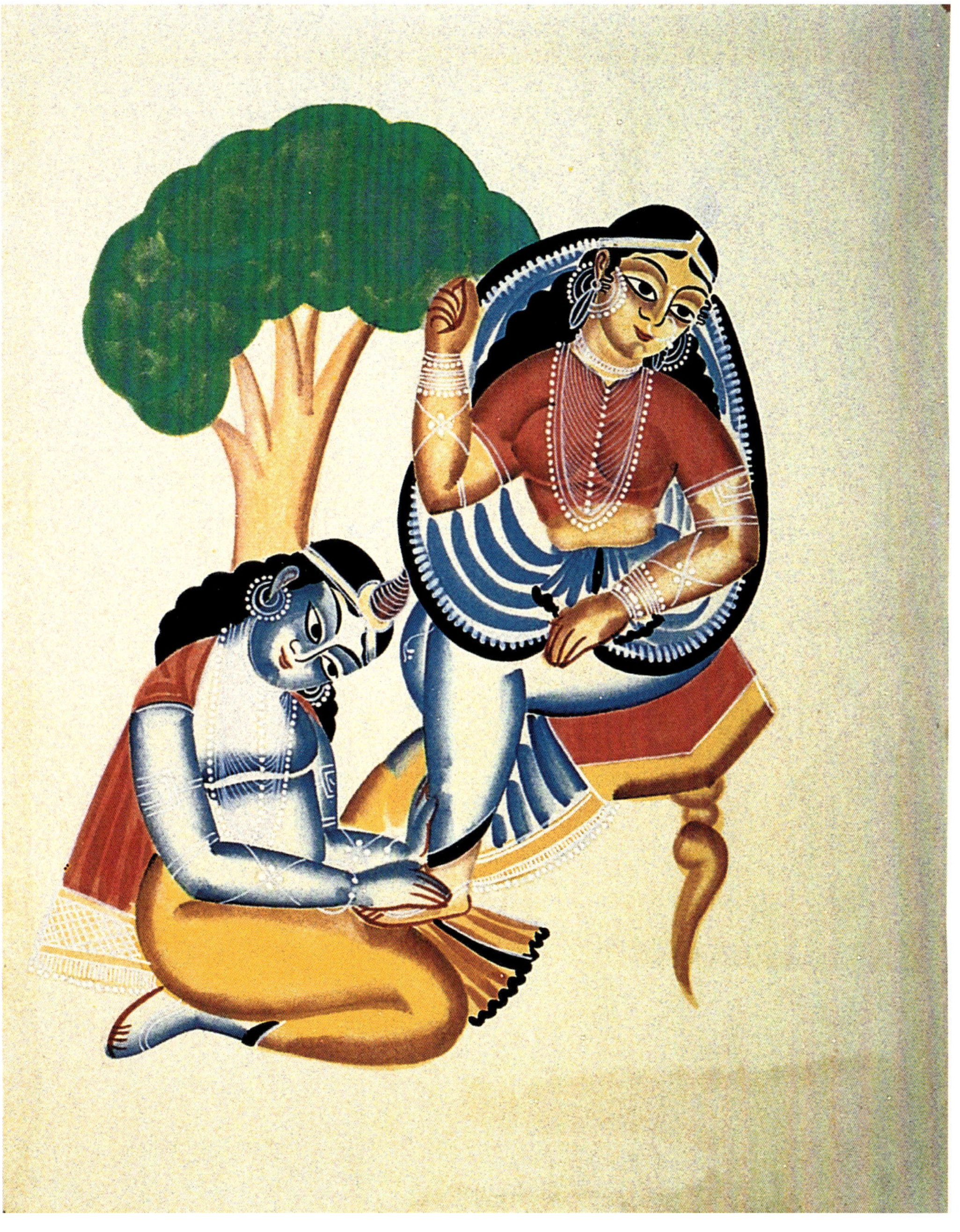

Kalighat painting, Kolkata, 20th century

forces that the Kalighat paintings emerged. The Kalighat painters portrayed courtesans with as much ease as they painted Radha, suggesting a crossover between the two; it is well to remember that it was here in Bengal that Radha was regarded as a *kalankini* or a defiled woman. One cannot but help in making this connection of the ambivalence of Radha when one sees Kalighat representations of Krishna. Here was a modern Krishna born in the courtyard of the dark and mystical Kali, seated on a chair and under a stylised kadamba tree instead of the idyllic Vrindavana, freed from the ethos of the *pata* or the scroll and therefore without a story to go with it but never lacking in layers of ancient myth, looking wistfully at Radha but without his flute. Simple, modern and yet not totally divorced from tradition, making his presence felt in the city which was a crucible of Indian modernity, the Kalighat Krishna is unique in the artistic expression of modern India, reminding its patrons that despite modernity the ancient was never too far off. It was here that the noted painter Jamini Roy found his inspiration and created his inimitable figures, making us realise that it is possible to be modern and Indian at the same time.

"While we are still in Bengal, let us go and see a village where they make horses," Vishwakarma said as they got into the chariot.
"Will I be able to ride a horse there?" Megha was very excited about being able to see horses as she was particularly fond of them.
"No, these are not horses for riding but are votive horses," Vishwakarma replied as he took the chariot up in the air and landed at Panchmura village in the district of Bankura.
"What are votive horses?" asked Megha.
"I will let the villagers explain it to you," Vishwakarma said.

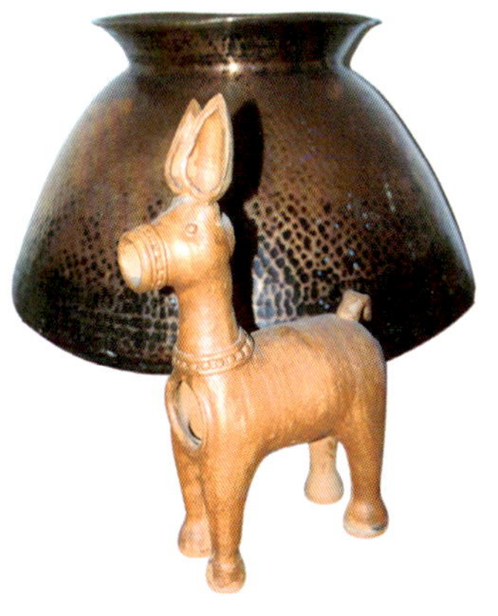

No sooner had they landed, a number of children gathered around the chariot and many surrounded Megha, hoping to play with her. Vishwakarma summoned Biswas, an elderly villager, and asked him to explain to Megha all about the horses. Biswas took Megha by the hand and accompanied her to an open space between four huts where a couple of women were at work.

"Horses are important to us for they are animals of great grace and speed. We make terracotta horses and place them under a tree, after which we chant prayers and ask for them be taken to our ancestors. Horses have been of significance to us from times ancient. In the Vedas horses were venerated and it was believed that the Sun god rode on a chariot driven by seven horses. They were trained to carry warriors and were indispensable in wars. Kings were very fond of horses and they were the pride of royal stables. But we are neither kings nor at war. We make these horses from the earth with faith and love and we are comforted in knowing that they will take our prayers speedily."

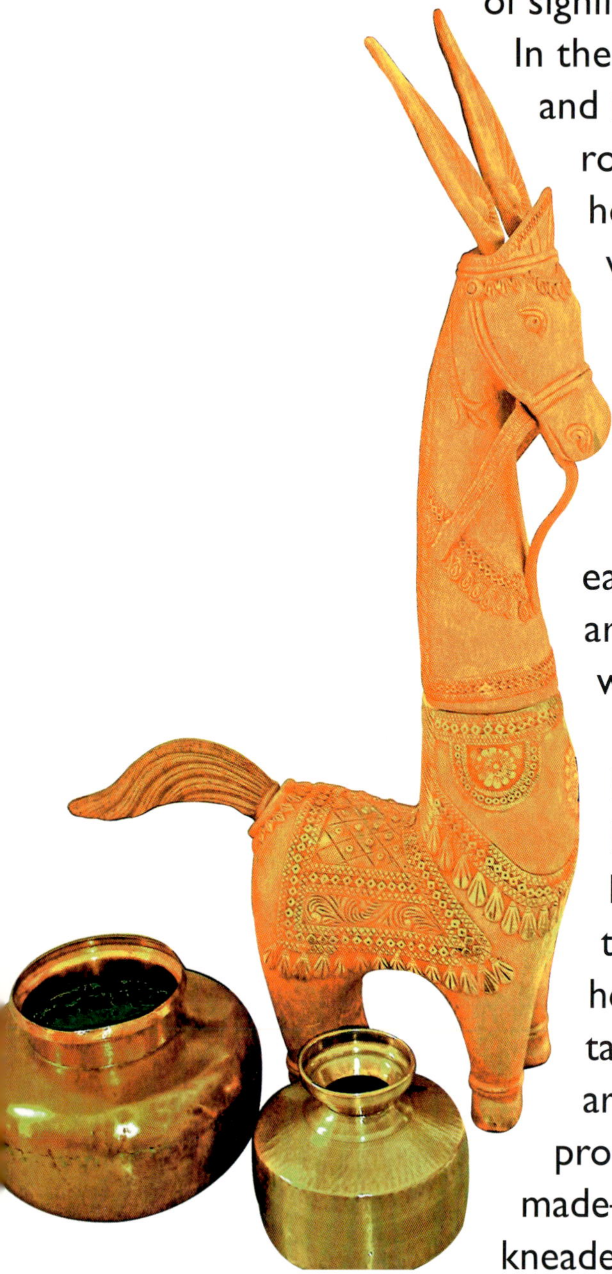

Megha was touched by what she heard. She now knew what votive horses were. She was particularly taken by the shape of the Bankura horse, with a long neck, a cute tail and elongated ears. She went around the village observing the process by which these horses were made—how the earth was collected, kneaded, shaped and finally decorated.

She asked if she could feel the earth. Biswas gave her a lump of earth and even as she held it he created a small Bankura horse for her. Megha was very pleased. "Be sure to leave it out in the sun for a day," Biswas told her. Vishwakarma signalled to Megha that it was time to go. Megha thanked Biswas and everyone in the village and promised that she would place the horse she had under a tree in her garden, and that she would also send a prayer with the horse to their ancestors.

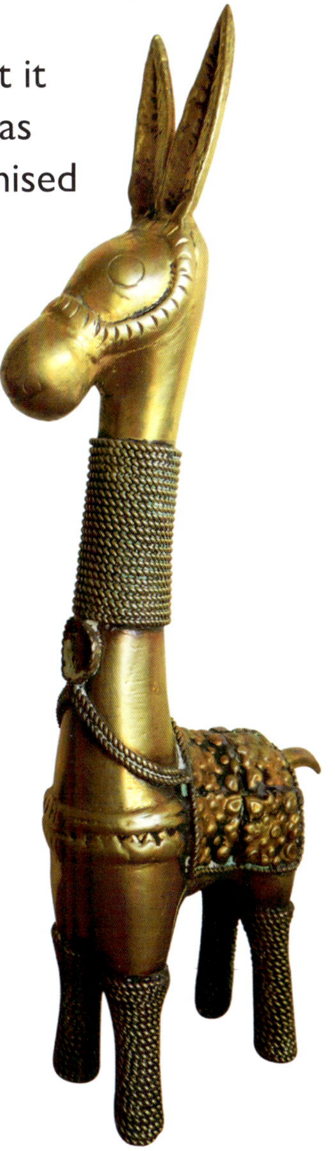

"Let us now go and meet some women in a small village who are busy embroidering fabric. This is a Bengali tradition where women in their spare time get together and embroider old and used saris. This is called kantha." Megha was most interested as she herself was learning how to embroider. After the chariot landed, Megha went towards a group of women who were sitting under a large banyan tree. They greeted her and she in turn folded her hands.

Soma was a middle-aged woman dressed in a cotton Shantiniketan sari, with the *pallu* over her right shoulder and a bunch of keys attached to its end. On seeing Megha she held her hand and welcomed her. "Let me tell you a little bit about kantha."

"A leisure time activity of the women of Bengal is an embroidery called kantha. Kantha means rags and traditionally, a number of worn-out saris are layered and sewn together with threads drawn out of borders of these saris. The entire field is then quilted into small blocks of different shapes using simple darning stitches. The piece is then embroidered using a variety of plant, animal and geometric motifs.

"Kantha takes its inspiration from both the *alpona* and tantric imagery of Bengal. Flowers and trees, animals and fishes, geometric and curvilinear patterns and the ever-present pan-Indian motif of the mango are very much a part of the floor diagrams of Bengal, which are a part of the vocabulary of every woman. These are then translated into the kantha. Wedding scenes, procession of musicians, local and Puranic legends, parrots and fishes, and the *shankh* and

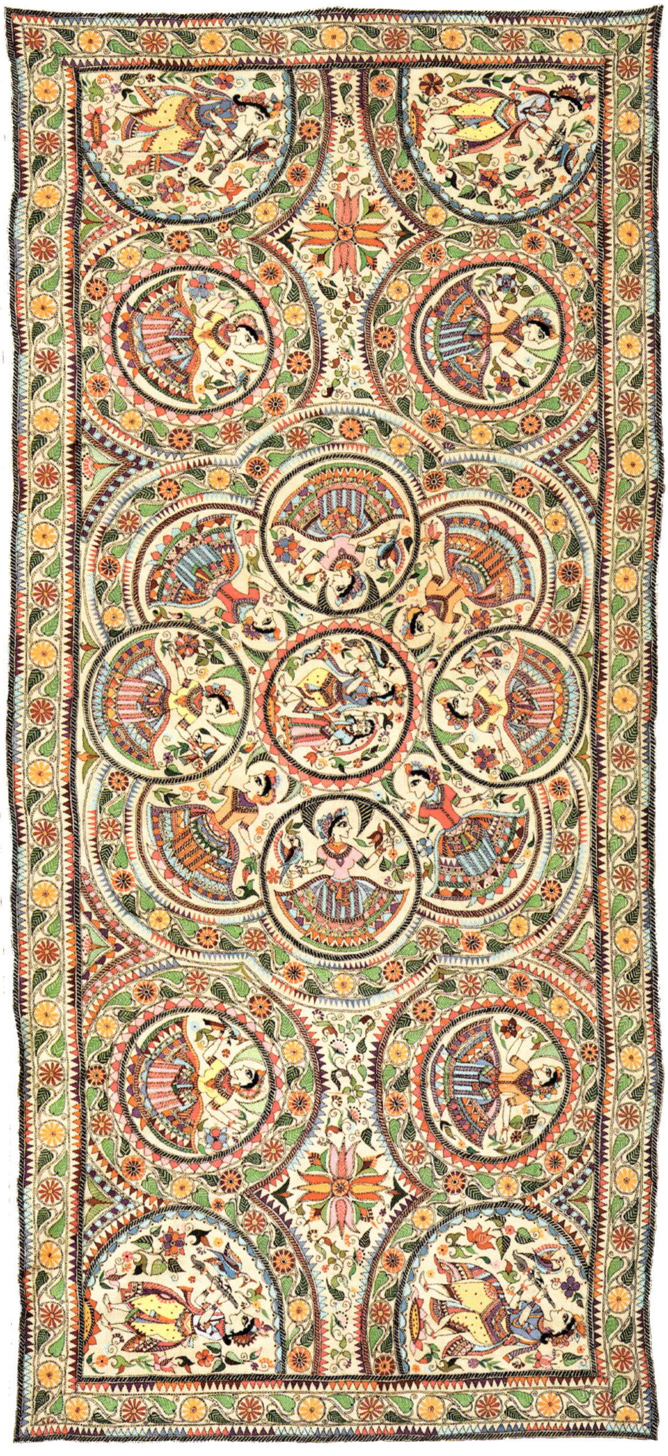

Krishna kantha

kalash are some of the common motifs. The motif of a central lotus radiating out in every direction, along with symbols of fertility like the fish and the bamboo, is a carry-over from the tanric yantras. Trees of life or *kalkas* are often placed in the four corners; Vaishnavite families place Krishna and Radha in the centre. Motifs from the world around, such as cars and trains, and people from all walks of life also find their place in kanthas.

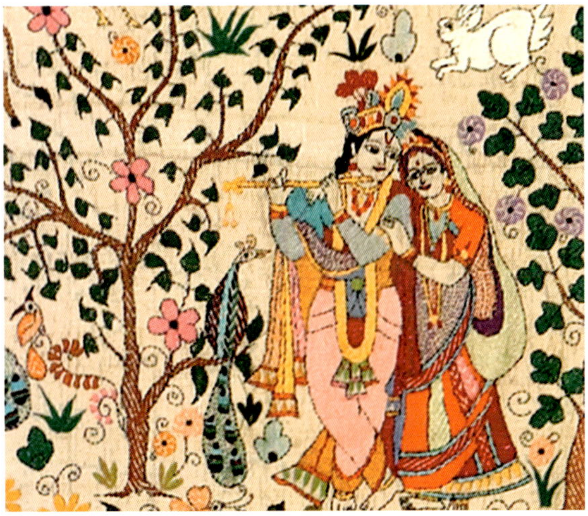

"The kantha is a work which gives wholeness to things that were of no use, to fragments that were without significance, and in doing so it not only creates something beautiful from what would have been discarded, but creates a fabric that gives warmth and comfort and brings with it the personality of the individual who creates it and also of the woman who used to wear that sari. A kantha is not just embroidery but carries with it voices of the women who make it.

"Kantha carries with it a message of wholeness, of making something out of fragments and therefore, brings with it a socio-economic as well as metaphysical symbolism. In not discarding worn out fabrics but making something new and beautiful out of it, Bengali women show their sense of thrift and frugality. In the joining of rags, kantha resonates with the robe of Buddha, which is a patchwork of rags and therefore represents the restoration of wholeness from tatters, or fullness or unification from momentariness.

"The kantha is an object of love, its symbols having universal validity. It is given as a gift and brings with it the wishes and experiences of the person who made it and is an assurance of protection and security. It is an expression and carries the voice of ancient memories, treasured ideals, family history and worldly aspirations of the ordinary woman of Bengal. Kanthas are an important part of the traditional embroidery of Bengal, and when Krishna appears in their creations, it carries with it the sweet love of Radha and the *gopis*."

Vishwakarma's chariot was now flying over Jagannath Puri. Megha looked down and she could see a lot of pilgrims. "This is one of the four main temples of Krishna in the country

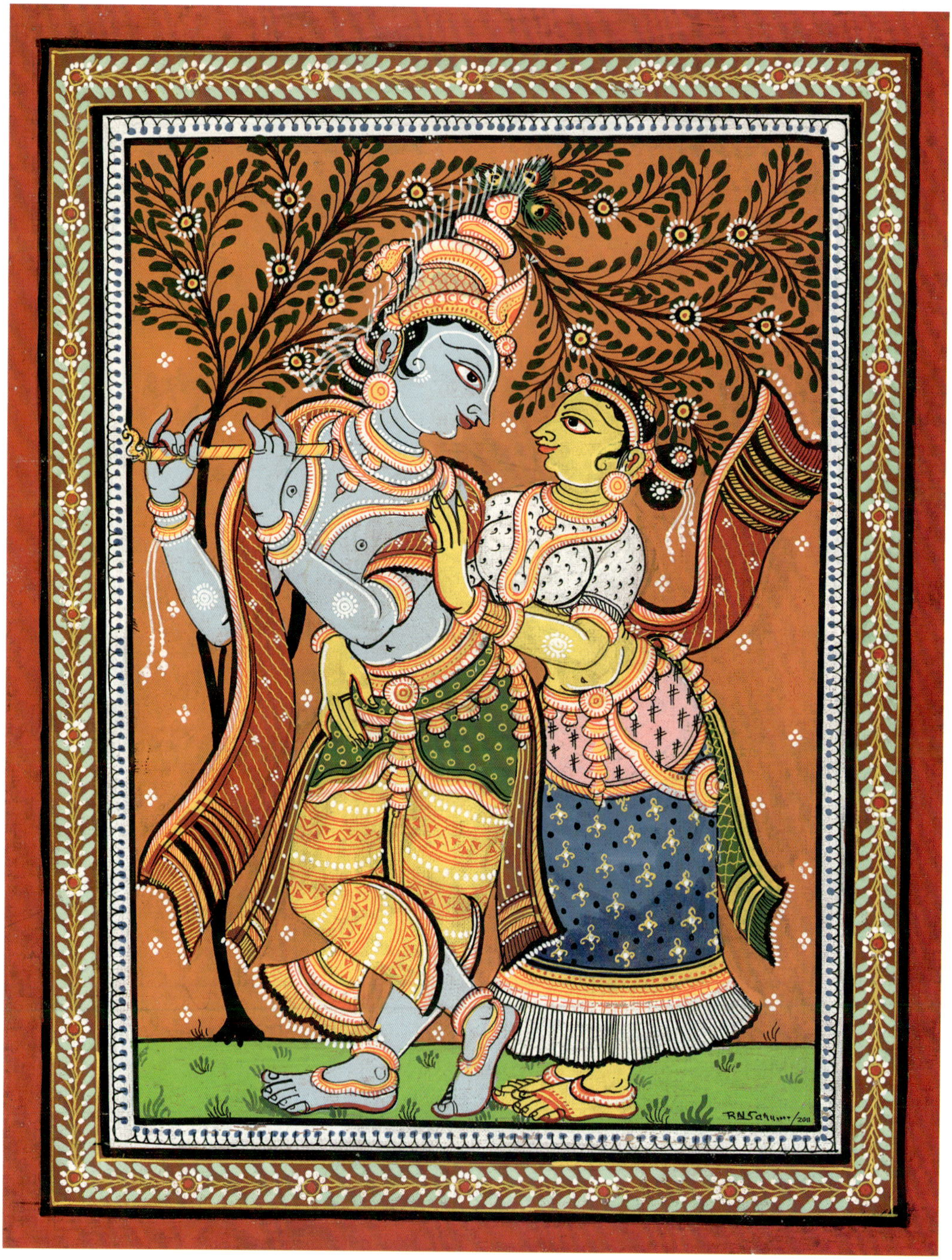

Patachitra, Odisha

and pilgrims come here from far and wide. An important festival here is the rath yatra where images of Jagannatha are taken out in a chariot. You must come here someday and participate in the festivities. But today I am taking you to a village called Raghurajpur, in which there is a colony of patachitra painters."

"What are these patachitras?" Megha asked, looking lovingly at Vishwakarma.
"I will let one of the artists explain."
As he finished speaking the chariot landed in Raghurajpur. It was a sleepy little village with a row of small houses. Cows were wandering about and leaves of neem trees fluttered. When the people saw Vishwakarma descend from the chariot they flocked to him and welcomed him with a garland of flowers. Vishwakarma in turn blessed them by putting his hand on their heads.

"What brings you here today, sir?" they asked.
"I have brought a young friend to you today. Her name is Megha and she wants to know all about patachitras."

The villagers spread blankets on the ground.
"Please rest here on this seat," and as Vishwakarma

sat, the women brought some milk and fruit for him and took Megha into their homes. Pranavda Sahu was a middle-aged man, dressed in a dhoti with a bare chest; his face was wrinkled and he had an inviting smile. He held Megha by the hand and spoke.

"The patachitra or traditional paintings of Odisha have a very special place in the arts of Krishna. A specialty of Krishna as Jagannath at Puri are the patachitras, which are done here at Raghurajpur. *Pata* is a piece of cloth prepared by applying a paste of black earth, cow dung or tamarind paste to ready the surface. The colours used in patachitras are made from natural ingredients such as china clay, chalk, conch shell and red stone. The patachitras of Odisha follow two main streams: that of Jagannatha, which portrays the trinity of Krishna, Balaram and Subhadra with their round staring eyes and handless arms, reminiscent of tribal figures. The other inspiration for the *pata chitrakars* of Odisha is the Chaitanya movement where Radha

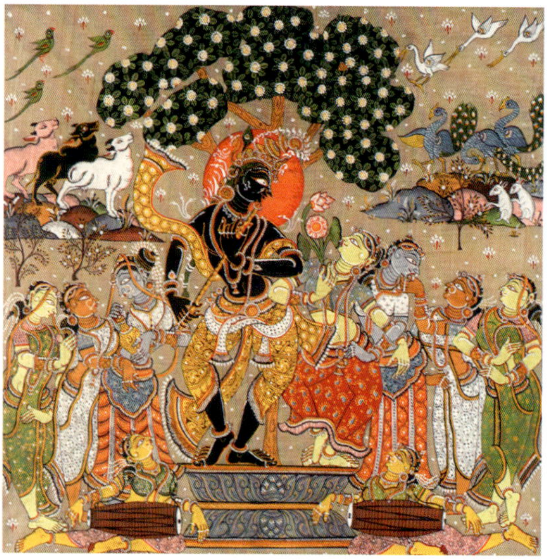

and Krishna are consorts and the romantic togetherness of the two is an important theme."

Megha listened with great attention and interest and wanted to see how the patachitras were made. Pranavda took her to his home and there she saw how the paper was treated and prepared for painting, the various colours and brushes that are used for the painting and she even tried her hand at drawing a little leaf on one of the paintings. There were a number of paintings of Jagannatha with the large circular eyes and two stumps for his arms. She asked Pranavda why Jagannatha looked different from the other images of Krishna that she had seen at home. Pranavda did not know the answer and told her that Vishwakarma would surely know.

Vishwakarma explained:

"The origins of Jagannatha are difficult to trace. Jagannatha is a derivation of a tribal deity and his worship combines many elements from tribal rituals. In the eleventh century, King Anantavarman Chodagangadeva of the Ganga dynasty built a great temple at Puri that rose seventy-five metres in height and rivalled any other temple in India. When he wanted to install an image of Krishna, he meditated to Brahma and soon he saw a log of wood floating down the river Mahanadi. The king approached me and wanted me to carve an image of Krishna on it. I agreed but on one condition—I be allowed to work without any disturbance. I and my sons started working and after many months Queen Gundicha became impatient and opened the room where I was working. Since she had broken the condition I left the image unfinished. That is why Krishna as Jagannatha has two stumps as his arms. I told the king that this image should be replaced every nineteen years.

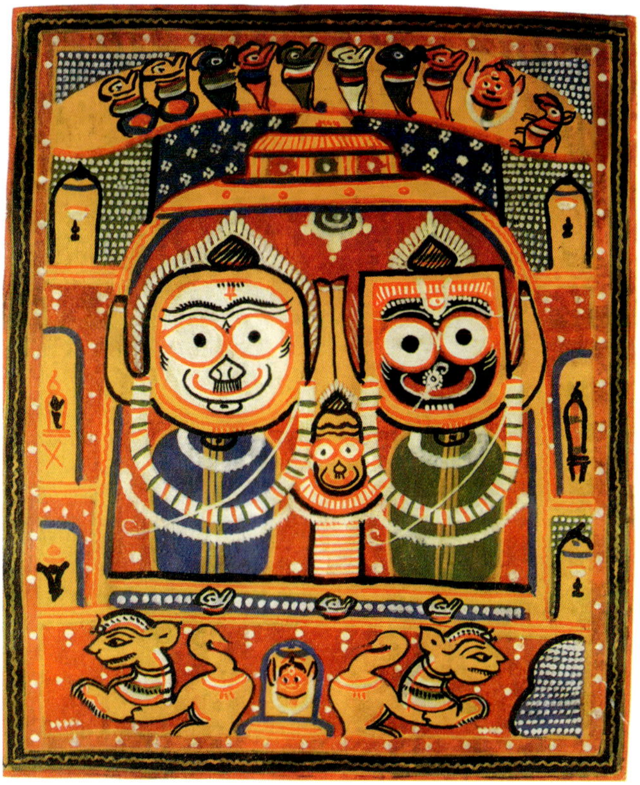

An elaborate and carefully orchestrated ritual spread over several weeks marks the making of these images. The first step is the identification of a tree from which the image will be made. Parties of priests and craftsmen are carefully selected and they set out towards the forest while chanting prayers. A neem tree showing divine signs is selected and a yajna is performed by the priests around the tree. The tree is then felled with ritual strokes, first from an axe of gold and then of silver, and the logs are carried back in a ceremonial procession and welcomed by throngs of devotees. Over a period of several days the images are fashioned from these logs by carpenters and craftsmen. These images are adorned and decorated and at every step prayers are offered for the successful completion of the task. Once installed, there is great rejoicing and celebration as Jagannatha stands once again in the temple, ready to bless his countless devotees for whom he is the Lord of the Universe."

Vishwakarma steered his chariot eastward towards the North East, the states known as the seven sisters. Turning to Megha he said that this was a very picturesque part of India with unique craft traditions. It was during the mid-sixteenth century that Prince Chilarai, brother of the king of

Cooch Behar, asked the Vaishnavite theologian Sankardeva to commission a great silk scroll depicting the life of Krishna. Sankardeva, who was responsible for bringing Vaishnavism to Assam, was not only a reformer but an artist as well. He asked the weavers of Barpeta in Assam to make a fabric depicting scenes of Krishna's life from the Bhagavata Purana, which was the central text for Sankardeva. This fabric was called Vrindavani *vastra*. It is said that it took twelve weavers more than a year to complete this task and this was presented to the prince in 1569, just before Sankardeva's death. Soon after its installation in the *satra* in Assam the fabric disappeared and it is believed that it found its way into Nepal and Tibet—probably travelling along trade routes—which was not only a trading partner with Assam but was a safe haven for many Hindu artefacts. What is interesting is that this *vastra* was used in those countries as lining for Buddhist tankas and also for ornamental clothes. It is important to note that the term *vastra* means both fabric and clothing.

The chariot landed at a *satra* in Majhuli, a island in the river Brahmaputra. As Vishwakarma and Megha stepped out, the monks greeted them

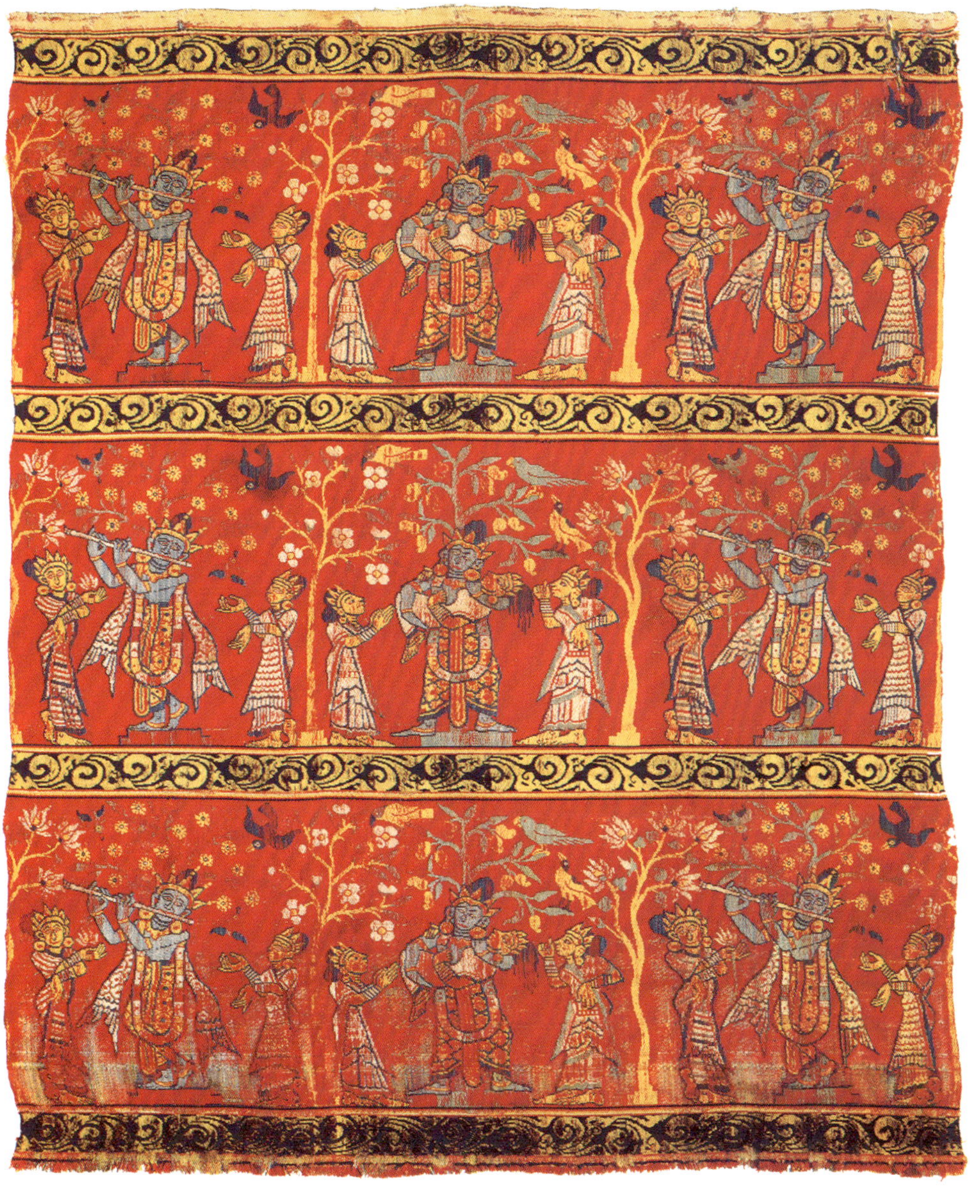

Vrindavani *vastra*, Assam, 19th century, Victoria & Albert Museum, London

and took them inside the beautiful monastery. Megha had never seen a monastery and looked all around. In the main hall a dance was being performed and in another corner some monks were reading a sacred scripture. One of the monks came towards Megha and spoke to her.

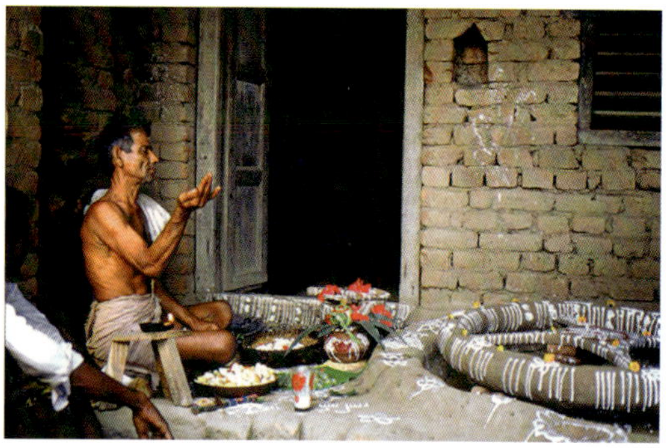

"Sankardeva undertook a twelve-year-long pilgrimage, mainly in the Braj country of Krishna, and later championed the teachings of the Bhagavata Purana in Assam. It was this text and not an icon that was the central object of worship in the *satras*. Sankardeva was a zealous Vaishnav and this did distance him from the pundits at the royal court of Assam. He established *satras* or monasteries and *namghars* or prayer halls. The *satra* housed monks but was also the centre of Krishna devotional songs, dances and plays. The Vrindavani *vastra* was used to cover the altar on which the Bhagavata Purana was placed, and also to cover the text and to drape the walls and ceiling of the *satra*. The *vastra* was also called *gosair kapoor* or a drape for priests and is similar to the present-day *gamusha*. The fabric, which was aesthetically pleasing, thus acquired a sacred status. In the sixteenth and seventeenth centuries the iconography on the fabric was complex, with a number of finely woven figures of the life of Krishna from the *dashama skanda* of the Bhagavata Purana along with some text, but with the passage of time and decline in the standards of weaving the figures became coarser and bigger. The most common motifs were *kaliya mardan* and *bakasura mardan* and also the *cheer harana* episode. The various avataras of Vishnu were also woven. Many of the woven figures in the *vastra* are similar to the figures drawn on the murals of the *satras*, suggesting that the artist for both may have been the same. In addition to the figures words were also woven into the fabrics and it is believed that these were from the songs composed by Sankardeva. The iconography of the *satras*, both in the murals and the *vastra*, drew from the *pala* traditions of Bengal and the western Indian traditions of Gujarat. The Vrindavani *vastra* is an important fabric of the Vaishnavas and remains the oldest surviving fabric of this tradition."

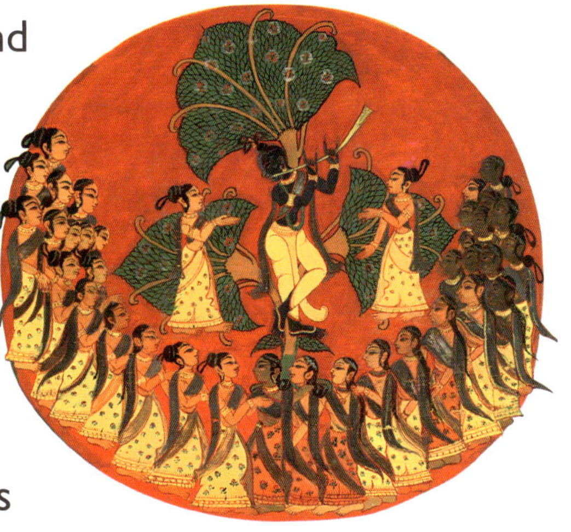

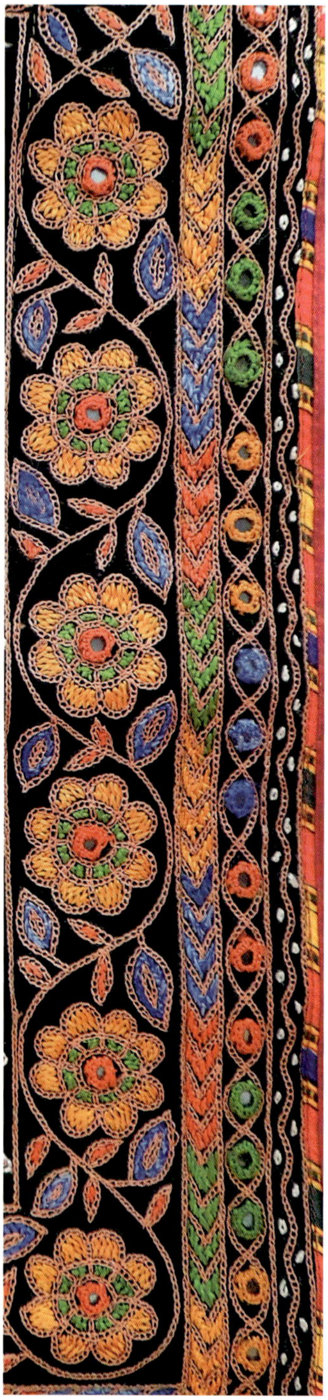

It was time to go southwards and explore the many different crafts in that part of India. Megha looked below and saw a huge and magnificent temple.

"That is the Brihadeshwara Temple in Thanjavur. Rising fourteen storeys into the sky it is more than a thousand years old and one of the most magnificent celebrations of Shiva."

Vishwakarma brought the chariot down in a small street in Thanjavur. The great temple was visible in the background and the small lane leading up to it was beautified with *kolams* outside each house. Devotees were returning from the temple with copper plates in their hands with prasada that they got from the temple: flowers, coconut and some rice. They saluted Vishwakarma and he in turn blessed them. Vishwakarma said pointing to the temple:

"With the history of a thousand years written in its temples and the footfalls of dynasties still heard in the soil, Tanjore or Thanjavur is the cultural capital of Tamil Nadu. Thanjavur flourished during the reign of Raja Raja Chola who built the magnificent Brihadeshwara Temple. Thanjavur also has the Saraswati Mahal library which is home to several rare manuscripts. The noted Carnatic musician Thyagaraja was born in Thanjavur district."

Megha looked at the temple and was wonderstruck at its beauty.

"Come and meet Shri Subramanian. He is a glass painter."

They entered a small shop where the walls were lined with a number of glass paintings. Pointing to these Subramanian said:

"The Tanjore style of paintings were popular during the seventeenth to nineteenth centuries under the patronage of Maratha rulers Sarbhoji and Shivaji, and in Mysore under Mummadi Krishnaraja Wodeyar. Tanjore painting was done on glass, which was popular in seventeenth-century Europe and spread from there to China and then India. Tanjore art was the product of a people who turned to the gods and goddesses for solace and assertion of their identity when the native rulers sold themselves to the British. It was under these circumstances that the Tanjore artist turned to glass painting. The most striking feature of these paintings is the use of gold leaf and gems. The paintings are made on jackwood pasted with unbleached cloth to which a mixture of limestone, chalk powder, gum and honey are applied in layers. After the icons are drawn certain parts of the figures are raised with this paste. Once dry, the gems and beads are set and the gold leaf pressed onto the painting. The Tanjore figures are robust and plump and are more iconic than narrative. The Western impact on these paintings is seen in the drapery, lamps, furniture and certain architectural features but they retain a distinct indigenous richness of colour and design. In creating these paintings the Tanjore artist had shown their flair for adopting new techniques and imparting to them their own stamp. Navneeta Krishna is one of the popular figures for the Tanjore artists, although they show a variety of Puranic gods and goddesses and also the royalty and nobility. Tanjore paintings are decorative and pleasing and were not only popular with people who wanted them for worship or decoration but also for the British who wanted to take home souvenirs.

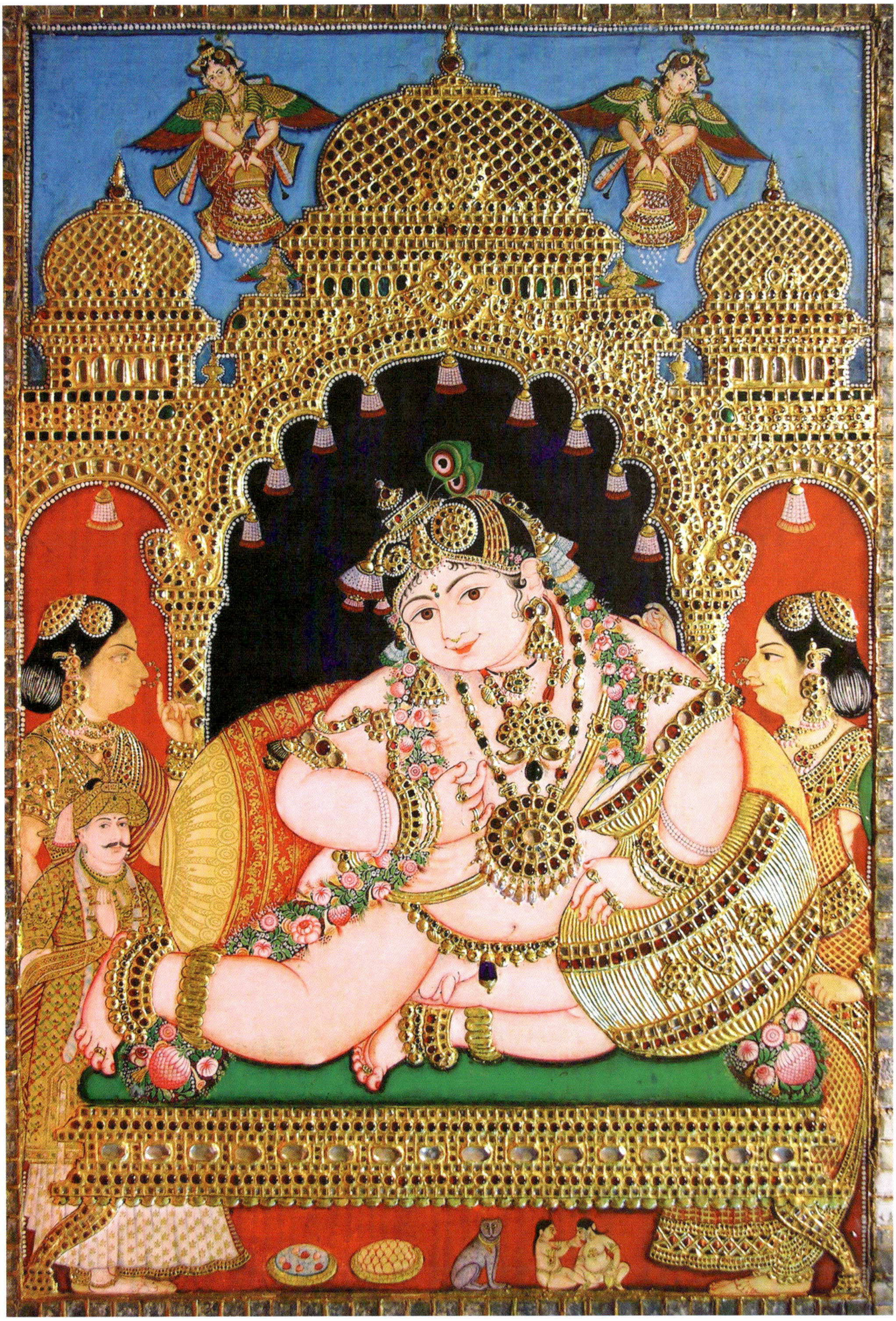

Tanjore glass painting, 20th century

Tanjore glass paintings became popular with the middle class in the Tamil country, who acquired them for decoration and even for worship. The Tanjore paintings are one of the last vestiges of traditional art in India before modern Indian art took over."

Megha looked at all the paintings but was most interested in that of baby Krishna. She asked if she could hold it and once permitted, admired it turning it back and forth. Looking at her Subramanian said: "Take it home. It is for you."

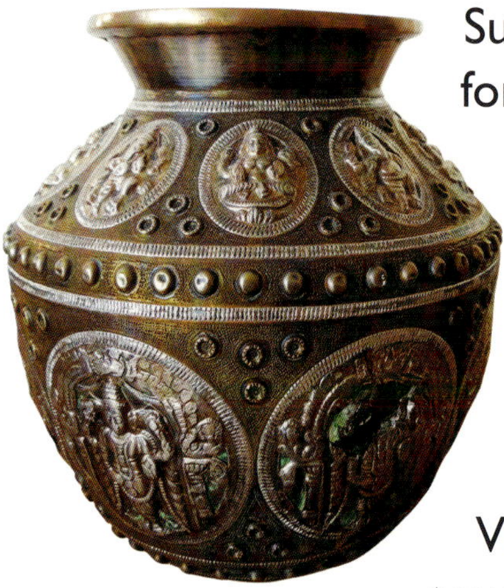

Megha looked at Vishwakarma and only after he gave her an approving look did she take the painting. "I will put it in the shrine at my home," she said.

Vishwakarma and Megha started walking towards the temple. There were many shops that sold a variety of artefacts. Vishwakarma took her to a particular shop which had a number of pots or lotas. "This is another noted craft of Thanjavur." He picked up a lota and showed it to Megha. It was a copper pot which had a number of images of gods and goddesses

done in silver. "Devotees place it in their home shrine. Some others take sacred water in it from places of pilgrimage."
Megha had never seen such a pot before. She held it and turned it around and it was as if she had a darshan of all the gods and goddesses, making her feel blessed.

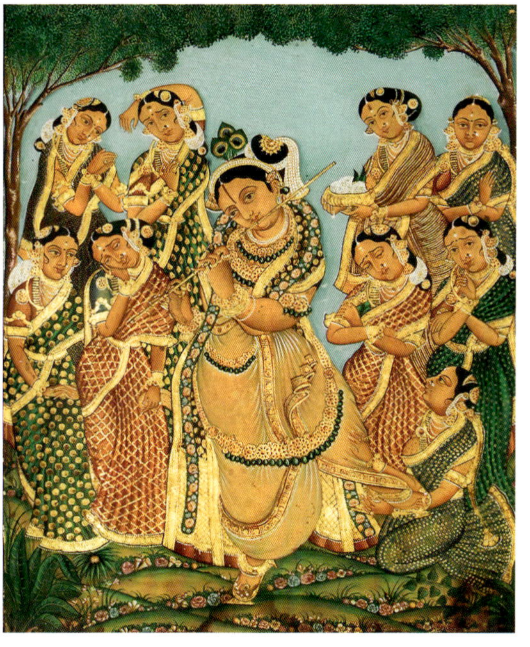

"You see Megha, there are so many ways in which we can meet our gods and goddesses even without going to a temple," Vishwakarma said as they climbed onto the chariot and took to the air. Flying southwards they came to Mahabalipuram and Vishwakarma brought the chariot down near the group of temples. Megha went around the temples but Vishwakarma beckoned her to come to an open stall where a number of workers were sculpting stone. Megha stood by one of the stone sculptors named Raghavan and watched in amazement as bit by bit and stroke by stroke, a beautiful image of Vishnu started to emerge from a block of stone.

She offered salutations to Raghavan and he spoke affectionately to her.

"Stone sculpting is a very old art and stones are ancient, millions of years old. It is as if these stones upon which we work carry within them the voice of our ancestors, in them are heard footfalls of our rishis of yore, in their patterns there is a memory of our forefathers who walked on this very earth, and in them is a primal rhythm. It is as if there is a silent story and a song within them and that is why we fashion our gods out of them. We have in our tradition ancient texts called *shilpa shastras* which contain rules and codes for sculpting and we follow them strictly. Our gods must be created with perfect measurements and even if we make a small mistake, we discard the image."

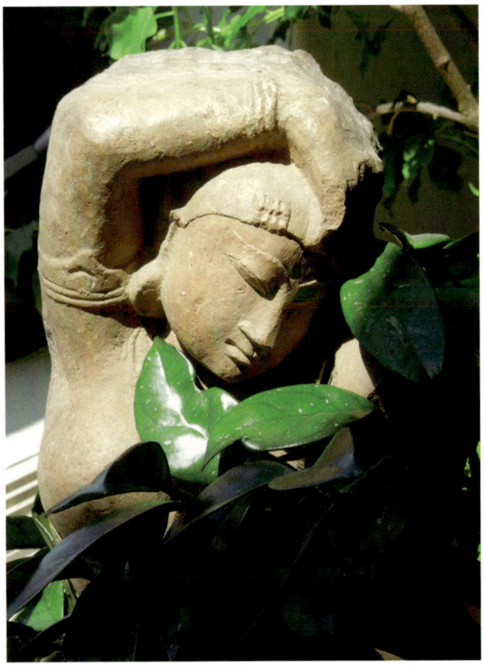

Raghavan pointed to a couple of images that had been thrown on the ground. Megha picked up an image and looked at it. "Why, it seems to be perfect to me."

"Look at the eyes. They are not as they should be and eyes are the most important part of an image. In them is the *shakti* or the strength of an image. You can have that *murti* if you like it."
Megha looked towards Vishwakarma and only when he nodded did she accept it. She thanked Raghavan and touched the *murti* to her forehead to receive blessings from it. As she got into the chariot, Vishwakarma explained to Megha all about the making of images, how they are installed in temples after they have been consecrated—a ceremony called *pranapratistha*—and how they have to be cared for after they are installed. "Once they are consecrated these *murtis* are considered to be alive and not inert. And when devotees look towards them, touch them and make offerings to them, the murtis respond to them with grace."
Megha clutched the *murti* that she got from Raghavan and decided to keep it in her home shrine and care for it.

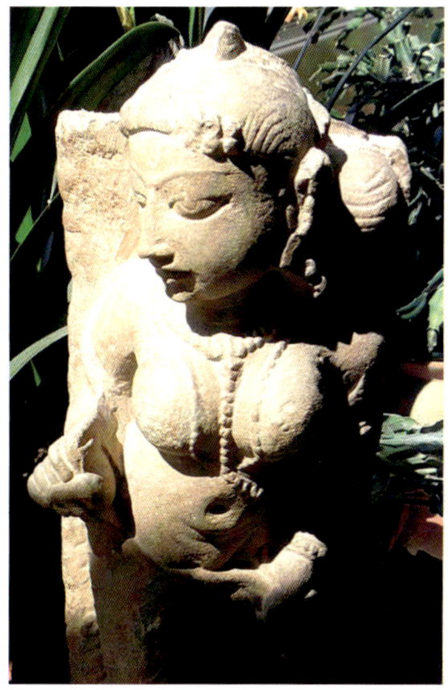

The chariot was flying over Andhra Pradesh and Vishwakarma pointed to the Char Minar of Hyderabad. He landed his chariot close to the monument and as Megha got out, she saw a lot of shops. There were many shops selling bangles and she asked Vishwakarma if she could go there. Vishwakarma took her to a shop with multicoloured bangles and introduced her to Salim. Salim offered his salaams to them and spoke: "Welcome to our shop. I have been selling bangles since I was a child. I used to go around the market singing *'choori walla choori, Radha ho ya Noori, rang be rangi choori, choori le lo choori'*. They are made in Ferozabad but we in Hyderabad sell a lot of them. *Choori* or bangles are at the very heart of a woman's adornment. The melody of their tinkling or *khanak* has had romantic connotations for ages. In ancient times a woman would intentionally make her bangles tinkle when she entered a room, particularly if her beloved was seated there. At weddings the bride would wear an armful of bangles. Bangles not only beautify the woman but bring her good luck and fortune. On special occasions like Eid or Karva Chauth women wear a lot of bangles, often offering them to goddess Mahalakshmi. In Bengal, women wear white bone bangles and in Kutch they wear thick ivory bangles."

Megha was fascinated by what she heard and saw at the bangle shop. She wanted to try on some bangles but there were none in her size. Salim

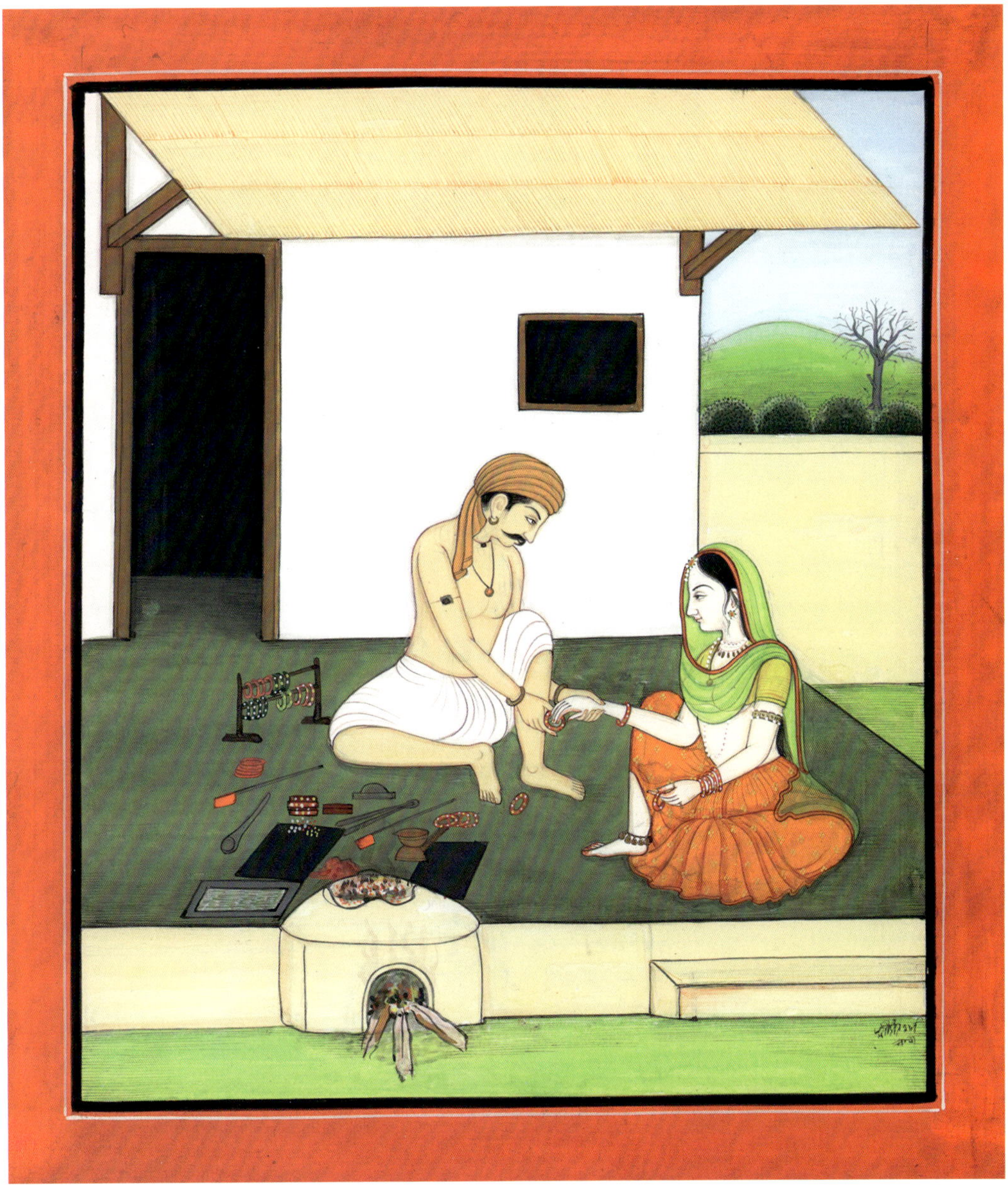

Bangle-seller

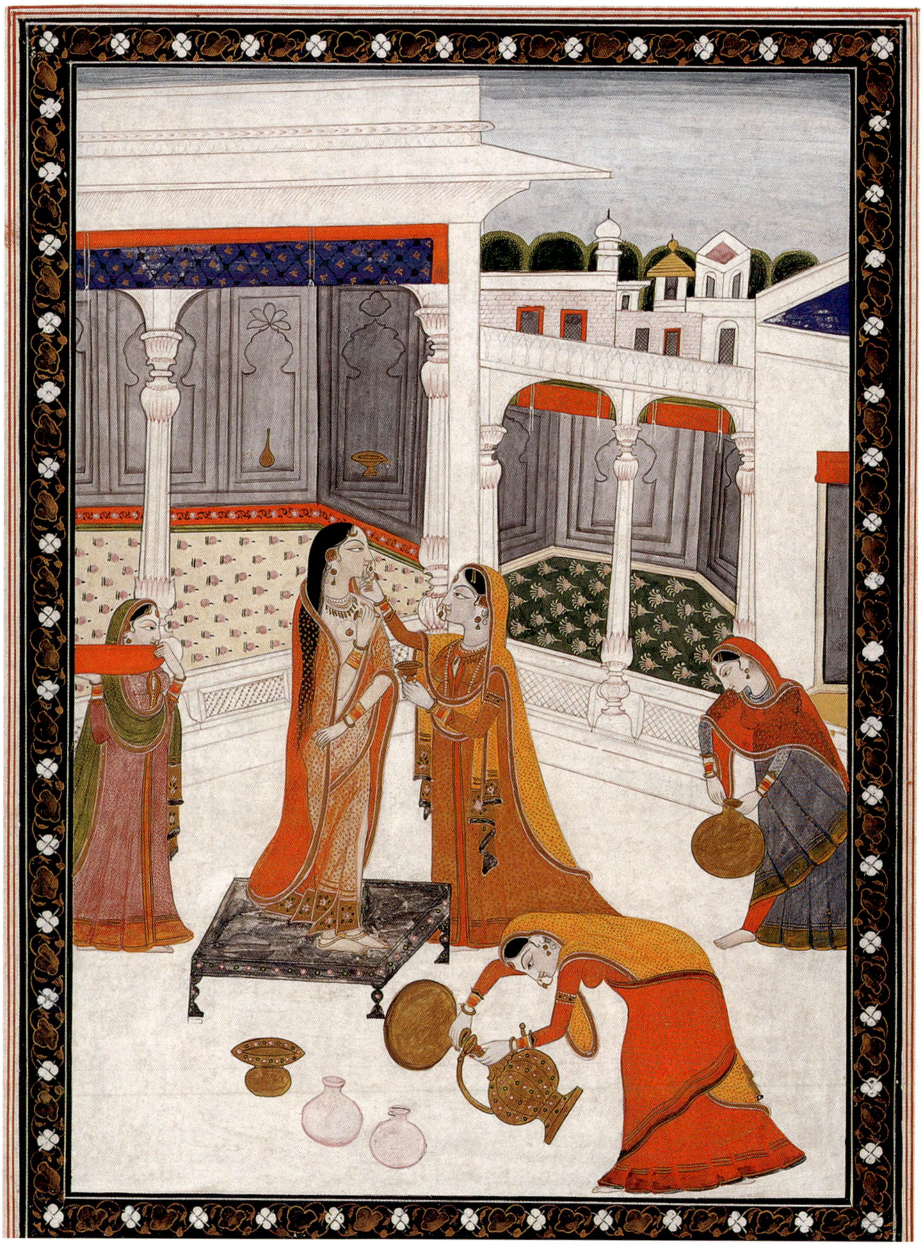

Adornment of a Nayika, Kangra, 1820–1830

went inside the shop and brought smaller bangles for her and as she put them on she showed her arm to Vishwakarma.

"You look like a bride! *Khush raho beti.*" said Salim. Hearing this Vishwakarma was pleased at how gracious and loving Salim was. He felt that the beautiful crafts of India bridged the gap between Hindus and Muslims, for colours and sounds, textures and shapes, the blossoms and the birds, and everything beautiful that human hands create were above religion and caste. The creation and the enjoyment of crafts was like a religion in itself. Before their journey was over, Vishwakarma mused, he will explain this to Megha and teach her through crafts that what is beautiful knows no religion.

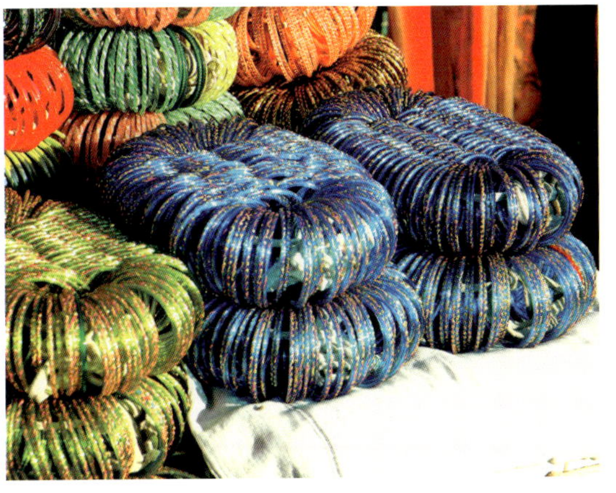

"Let me now take you to see a craft of Andhra Pradesh," Vishwakarma said taking control of the chariot.
"And what will that be?" Megha was never too tired to learn about another craft and the people who made it.

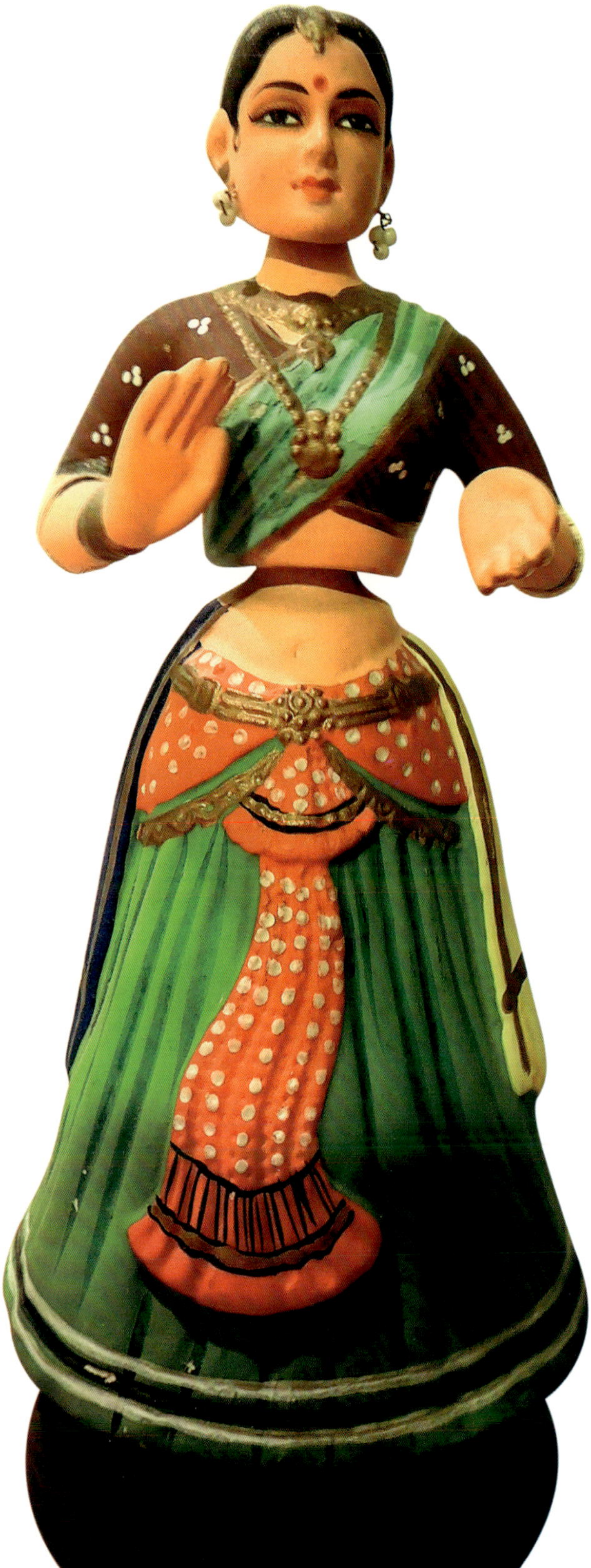

Dancing doll from Andhra

"I want to take you to Srikalahasti to meet a family that does kalamkari."
"And what is kalamkari?" she asked.
"Let me tell you even before we get there."
Vishwakarma kept flying the chariot and spoke simultaneously.

"Kalamkari or pen work refers to textiles that are printed or painted using a particular technique. Modern kalamkari can be traced to seventeenth-century Andhra Pradesh and, like most other Indian arts, owes its birth to temple rituals. Kalamkari textiles were used as aids to storytelling in temple precents. While the motifs of kalamkari are drawn from Hindu mythology, it owes a lot to Persian influences which came into this area when trade links were established between the Safavid dynasty of Persia and the Qutb Shahi dynasty in Golconda. The two centres of kalamkari are Masulipatnam and Srikalahasti. Kalamkari textiles were used to decorate temples and palaces as well as for narrative scrolls, but over the years they have been used for household purposes like furnishings and even clothing. In British India, kalamkari fabrics were particularly popular as bed covers and came to be called *palangposh* or palampore.

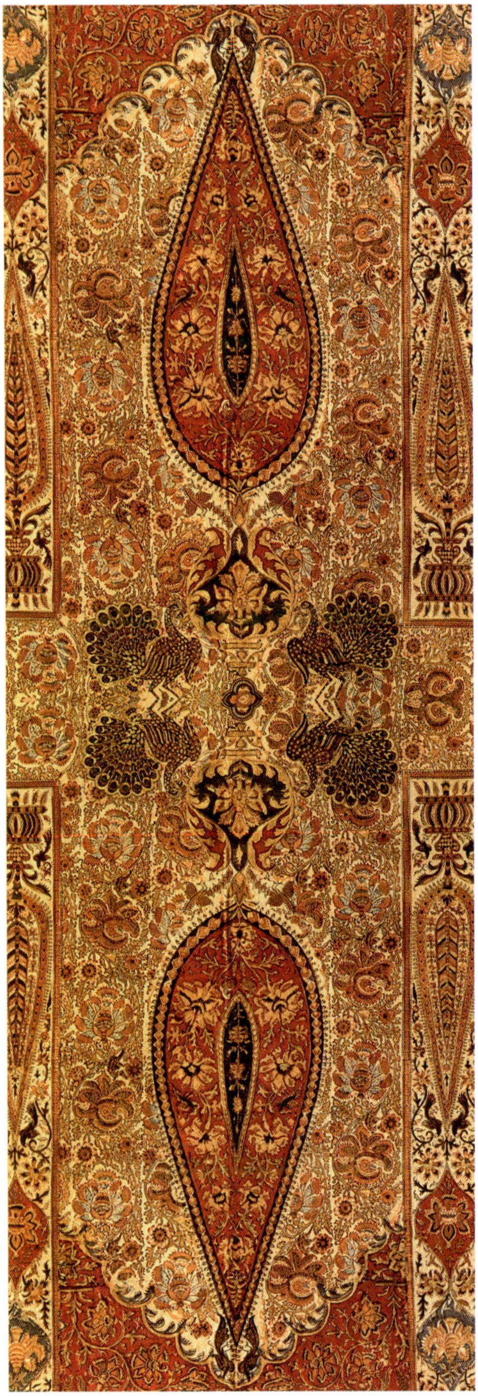

"The procedure for producing a kalamkari starts with preparing the cloth, which is first bleached and then soaked in myrobalan solution mixed with fresh buffalo milk. The outlines are then drawn in red and black. The cloth is washed in running water before sunrise, starched and waxed. The pen or *kalam* is made of a bamboo stick, at the end of which a thick pad of human hair is attached and figures are drawn with this pen or, alternatively, a wooden block. Red, blue, yellow and green are the main colours that are used. Kalamkari artists worked with the techniques of a mural painter and the usual themes were taken from the Puranas as well as from the *Mahabharata* and *Ramayana*. The kalamkars were able to produce two-dimensional figures that equalled temple sculptures and murals. Kalamkari textiles thrived on Muslim court patronage, Persian trade and the markets of Europe, and remain even today an important part of the craft traditions of India."

Vishwakarma landed his chariot in a field where Narasimhachari and his family were working on indigo. On seeing Vishwakarma the oldest brother came to receive them and folding his hands said, "Welcome sir to our home. We feel blessed to see you."

"I have brought a special guest to meet you. This is Megha and she wants to know all about kalamkari."

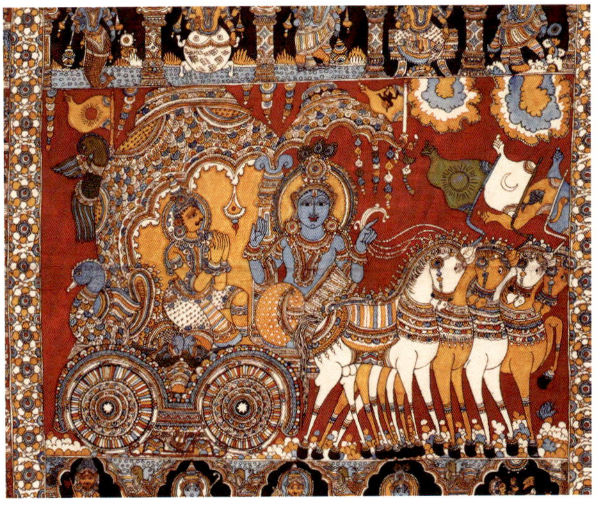

"Of course, it will be our pleasure." Saying so he held Megha's hand and took her to the indigo processing facility.

"The colour blue is very important to us for we need it to make figures of Krishna and Vishnu. To make that colour we take leaves from the indigo plant, boil them and let it stand overnight. The next morning we jump into the mixture and mix it with our feet till the perfect shade of blue is obtained. We then boil it again and make cakes of the dye. And then when we want to apply the colour blue we dissolve the cake in water and dip the clothes in it. Did you

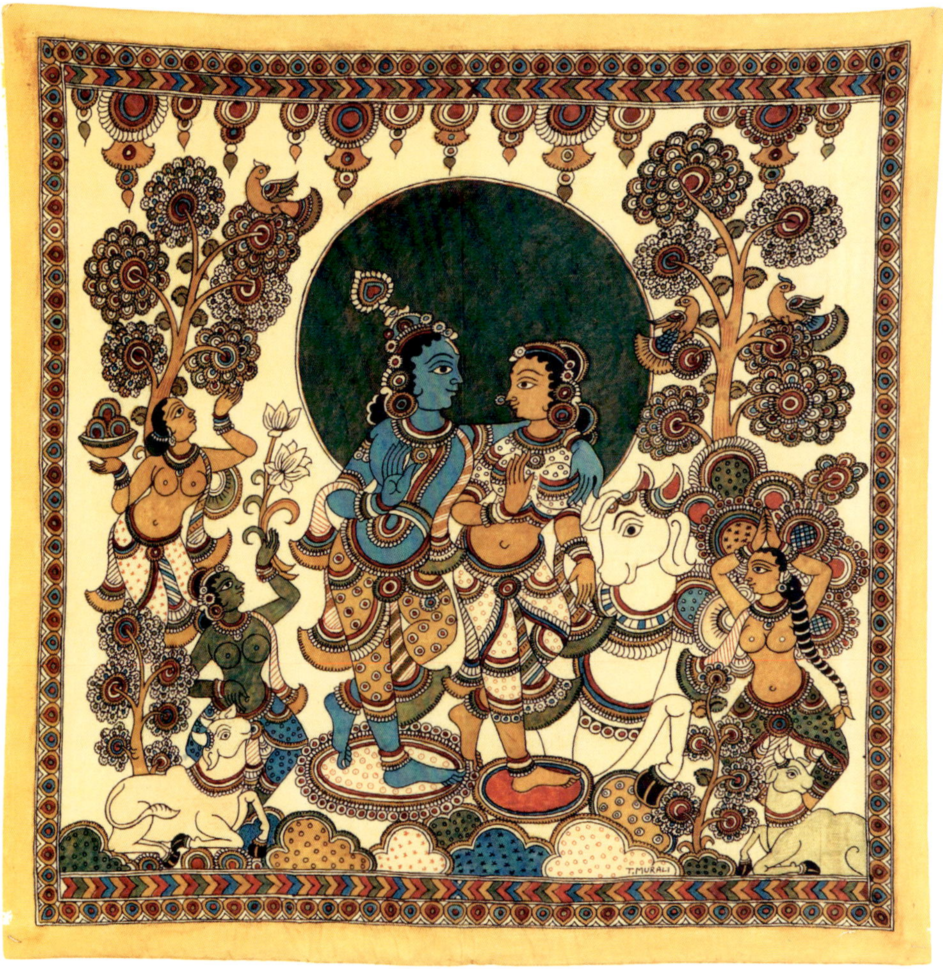

Kalamkari, Andhra, 20th century

know that for many years we were the only people in India who were able to make the colour blue from the indigo plant?"

Megha was listening attentively. She had a blue kurta at home and she wondered if it had come from here.

Vishwakarma, who was watching from a distance, intervened and spoke to Megha. "The indigo plant played an important role in our freedom struggle. Since it was the only source of the colour blue, textile workers in England wanted it and the British, who were our rulers, asked the farmers in Bihar to plant Indigo instead of rice. This led to a famine and many people died. Mahatma Gandhi was so touched by this that he led a campaign against it."

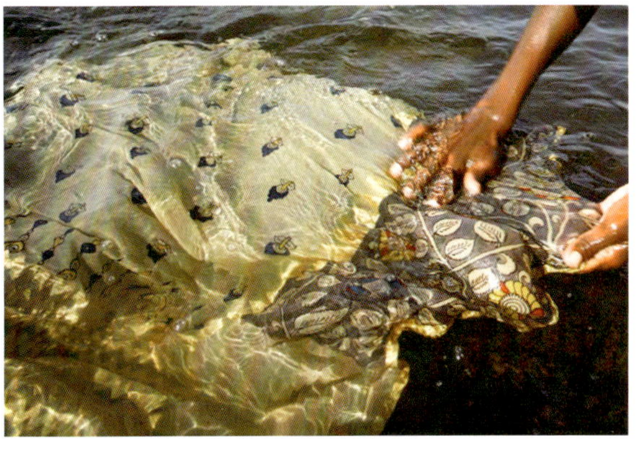

Megha was happy to have learnt this lesson from Indian history even as she understood what kalamkari was. Narasimha insisted that Megha and Vishwakarma have a meal with them and took them into his house where food was served on banana leaves. This was a new experience for Megha and she was touched by how everyone in the family—young and old, men and women and children—participated in the making of kalamkari. Before they left, Narasimha gave Megha a small kalamkari piece which had Radha and Krishna painted on it. Vishwakarma blessed Narasimha and turning to Megha, said:

"Since we are already in Andhra, I want to take you to Cherial, a village of traditional scroll painters. You are now familiar with kalamkari so let us go and meet these scroll painters who paint in the kalamkari style. They also draw inspiration from the wall paintings of the temple at Lepakshi." Vishwakarma steered his chariot towards Cherial.

As it happens, an old man was painting a scroll and on seeing Vishwakarma he got up and folded his hands, inviting both of them to his home. Vishwakarma explained why he had come. Ramakrishna spoke in a hushed voice as a newly painted scroll was being given to the singers and they were performing puja.

"The Deccan is known for its kalamkari paintings on textiles and for its wall paintings at Lepakshi.

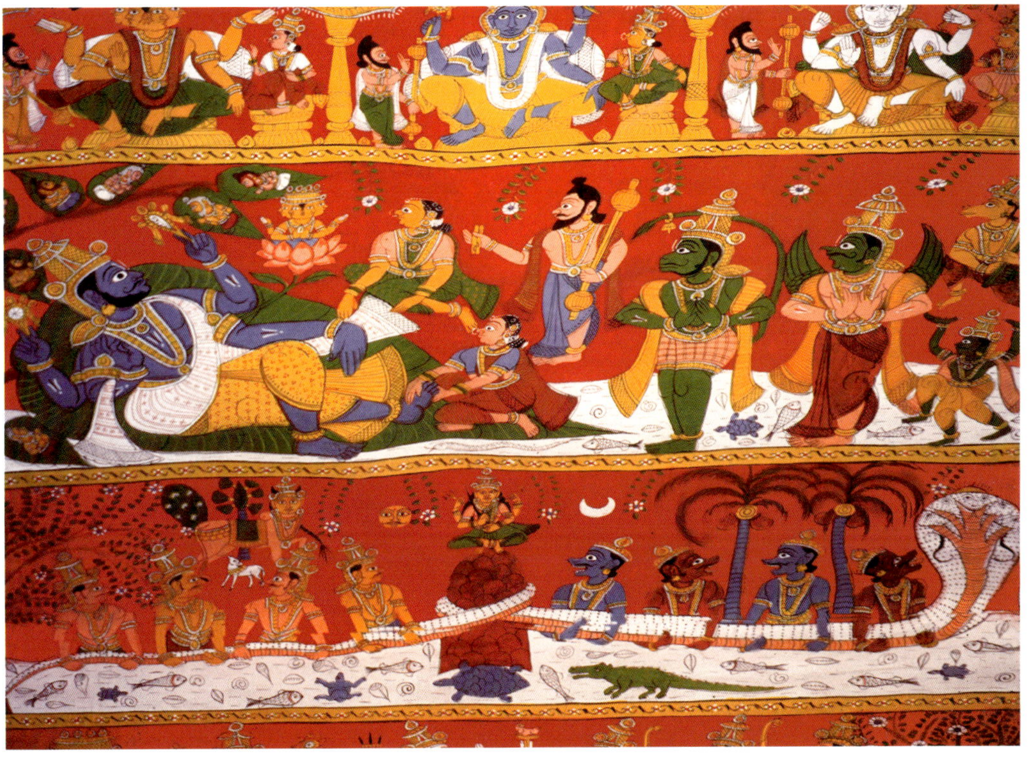

Vaishnava scroll, Andhra, 18th century, Jagdish and Kamla Mittal Museum, Hyderabad

Recently, scroll paintings from the Deccan have come to light. While the Deccani scrolls depict Hindu mythological stories, a narrative of special interest to these painters is the story of Markandeya and Bhavana rishis. Rishi Markandeya performed a yajna to provide clothing for the gods. From the sacrificial fire rose Bhavana rishi and he pulled a fibre from the lotus stalk that rose from Vishnu's navel. He made a ball of thread from the fibre and under Vishnu's direction, used this thread to make clothes for the devas. Bhavana married Bhadravati, daughter of Surya, who bore him hundred and one sons and from whom came the Padmasalis and Pattusalis, the original weavers from Andhra. Telangana scrolls of the eighteenth century were strongly influenced by the Vijayanagara styles of painting while the scrolls of the nineteenth century show features of Nayaka art and were produced under the patronage of Hindu zamindars. The fabric for the scroll is prepared by applying several layers of white kaolin to which starch and gum were added. The fabric is then burnished with a polished stone.

"Gum from the tirman tree was used as the binding medium for colours. Red is the predominant colour for the background. The

Telangana scrolls are characterised by the vigour of the figures and a persistent regard for a certain rhythm which linked the entire scroll. When completed, the scrolls were given to itinerant singers and performers who narrated the story painted in the scroll. The scrolls had a strong caste orientation and each caste governed the general layout of the scroll."

Ramakrishna unrolled a large scroll while Megha watched in silent admiration.

From Andhra Pradesh it was only a hop, skip and jump to Kerala. Vishwakarma steered his chariot westward and landed in a small town called Aranmula.
"I want you to see the deity in the temple here and then I will tell you a little story." Vishwakarma said.

Megha got down from the chariot and walked towards the temple, took her shoes off, rang the temple bell and saw the deity in the temple. She did not know who it was but none the less she folded her hands out of reverence, applied kumkum from a small cup left by the side and went back to the chariot.

Vishwakarma held her hand and said, "Many years ago in this small town there was a temple and a community of priests and devotees who had settled around it. The head priest of the Aranmula temple allowed a group of metal workers to settle on temple lands and make lamps and utensils for the temple rituals. However, when they made these metal objects, they turned out to be of very poor quality and the priest threatened to evict them. Women of these artisan families were particularly distressed and threw their ornaments into the furnace. The metal objects that resulted from this act turned out to have a particularly bright sheen and looked almost like mirrors. The priest asked the artisans to stay on and make a crown for the icon in the temple. The crown indeed shone like a mirror and the deity is still called the mirror deity. The artisans then started making shining mirrors of metal and they are known today as Aranmula mirrors."

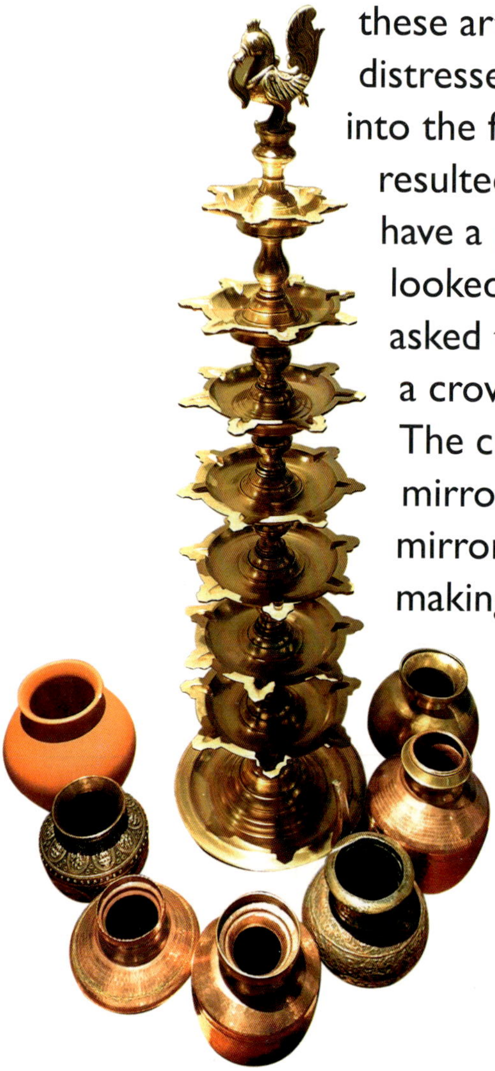

Megha was delighted to hear the story of the Aranmula mirror.

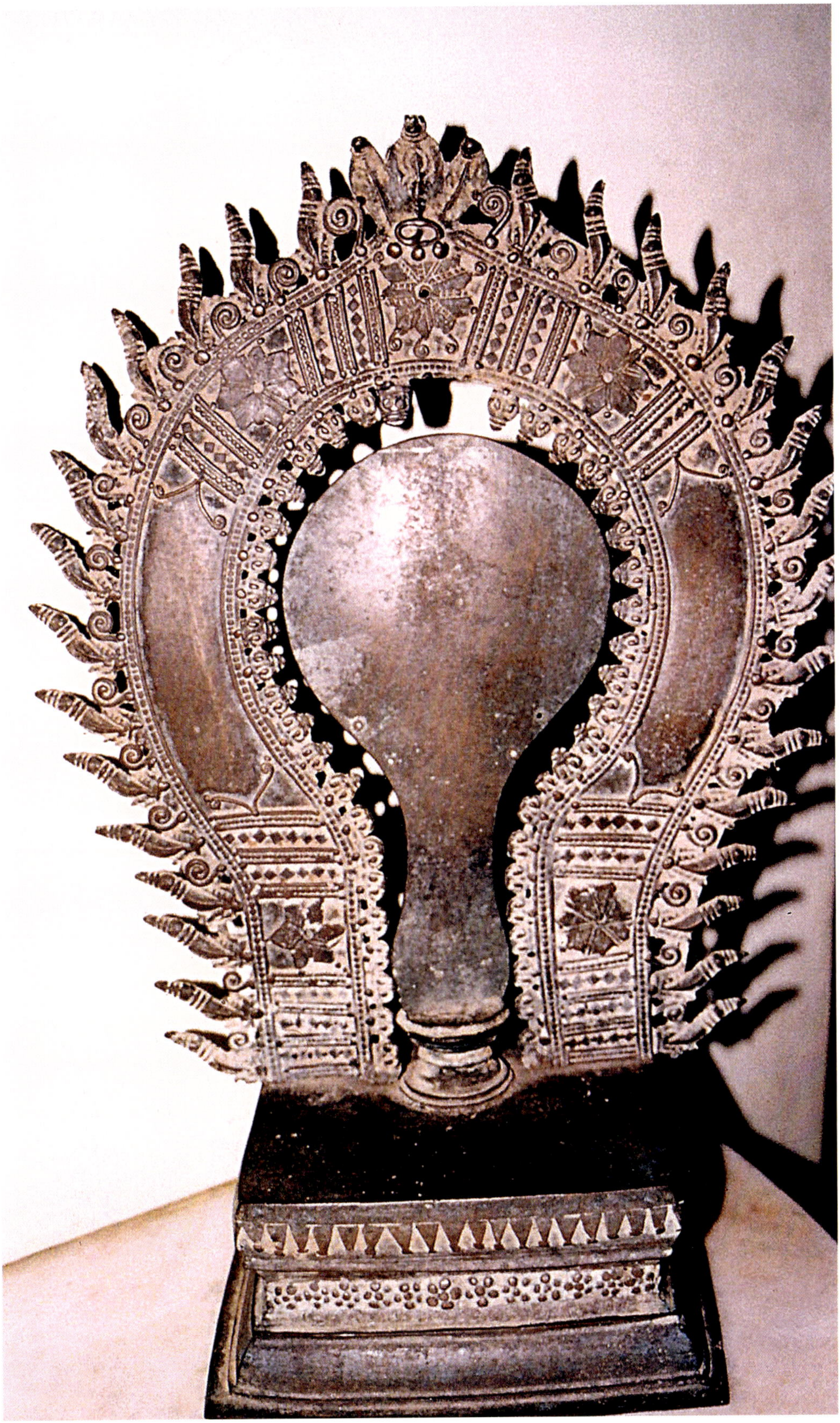

Aranmula mirror, 19th century

It was time to go northward and the first state was Karnataka. Vishwakarma told Megha that Karnataka was home to many crafts but he particularly wanted to show her the craft of making wooden toys. Megha was most interested and got ready to get down as soon as the chariot landed in the small village of Channapatna. Krishnappa, a middle-aged man wearing a dhoti, was surprised to see Vishwakarma and escorted him to his home after offering salutations.

"Meet my young friend Megha. Please show her what you do." Vishwakarma requested.
"It will be my pleasure," Krishnappa responded.

Taking Megha by the hand he took her inside his workshop where a large amount of wood was stored.

"Ours is an ancient tradition, which was supported by kings and we were known as chitragars. We bring this wood from the forest and work on it with a lathe to make different toys, such as a horse or a swan or mini kitchen utensils. Then we paint them with lac and polish them. Toys made here are found all over India."

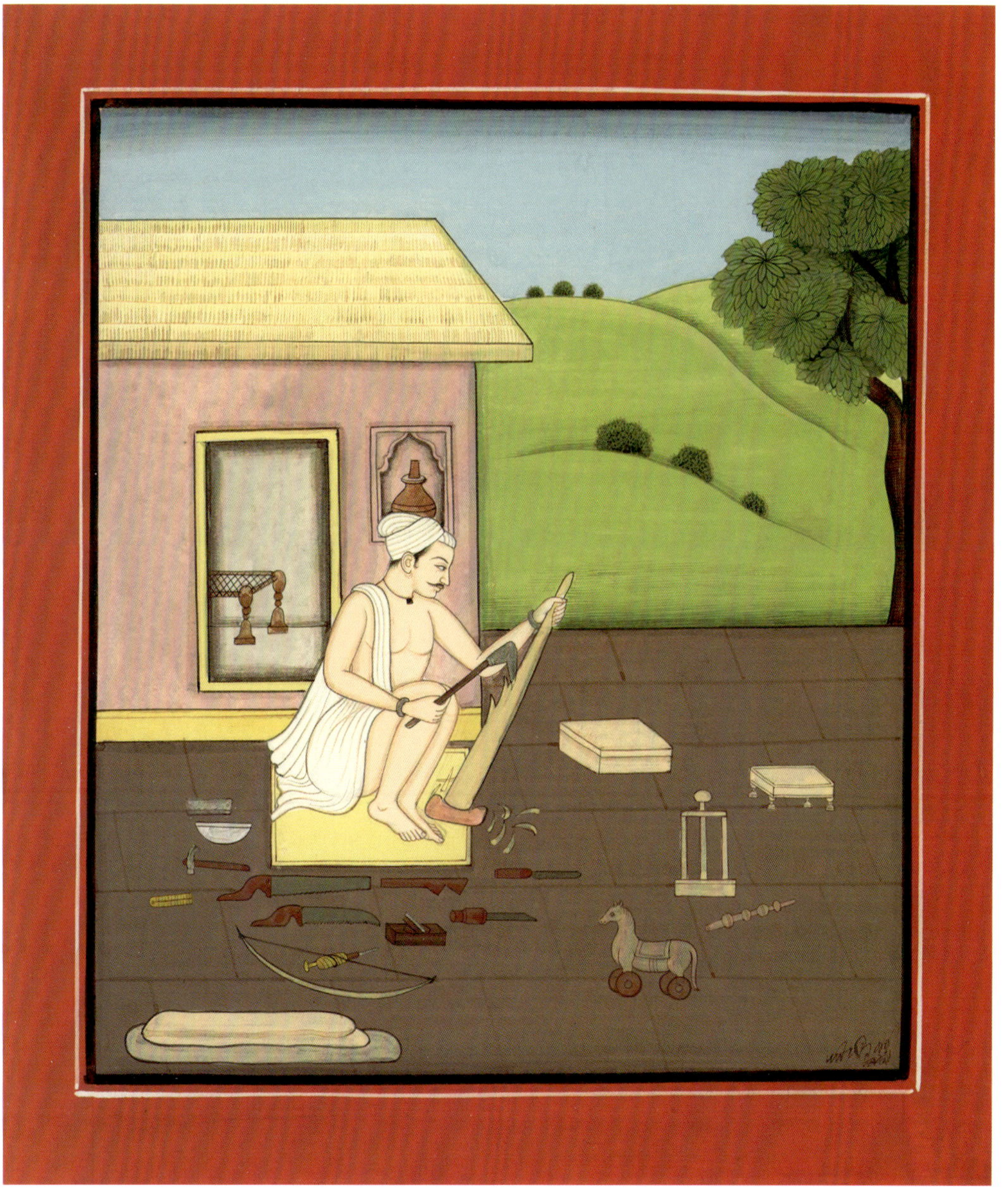

A woodworker, painting by Parikshit Sharma

Megha was particularly interested in the kitchen utensils and even before she could ask Krishnappa gave her some.

Megha was very thankful. Krishnappa's wife Yellamma gave her a big hug and as Megha turned around to go back to the chariot, she bid them goodbye with folded hands.

As they flew away in his chariot, Vishwakarma explained the importance of toys to Megha.
"Children grow up with toys and they make a significant impression on their growing minds. There is both magic and play in these toy, such that they become trusted companions and dear friends to the children."

Vishwakarma landed his chariot in Bidar in Karnataka. Across from a lush rice field was a small house where a person was polishing a metal *huqqa*.
"This is Venkat Rao and he works on what is called Bidriware," Vishwakarma said and holding Megha's hand, took her inside the house. Venkat greeted Vishwakarma and Megha and offered them a seat.
"Please do come and meet the rest of my family.

This is Usha, my daughter." Venkat took Megha by the hand into another room.

"Hello Usha, I am Megha. Please tell me about your craft. I would like to learn something about it," Megha said. Venkat held the *huqqa* and spoke. "It was in the fourteenth century that a sultan from the Bahamani kingdom in the Deccan invited Abdullah-bin-Kaiser from Persia to decorate his palace. Abdullah was a master craftsman and he knew how to work with metals.

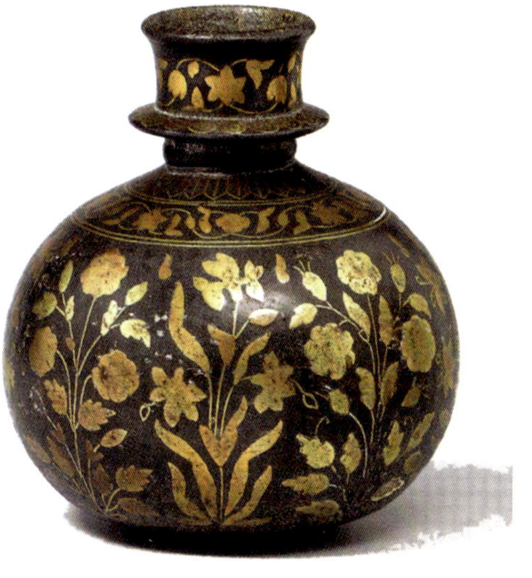

Huqqa base in Bidriwork

"He made an alloy of copper and zinc and poured it into an earthen mould. Then, once the object was formed, he took a metal stylus and etched designs into it—patterns like poppy flowers, floral vines, the moon and stars and also calligraphed words from the Qur'an. These designs were made with silver and the object was then polished with a special dust from the basement of a fort not far from his home. The sultans preferred objects like bowls for washing hands, water jugs and *huqqa* bases. They took this craft to Bidar and that is how it got its name—Bidri. Since then the craft has been handed down through succeeding generations, mostly among the local Muslim and Lingayat sects."

Megha touched and felt the *huqqa* and admired the pattern. Venkat gave her a small box that he had made. Megha thanked him, bid him goodbye and returned to the chariot. Vishwakarma blessed Venkat and manoeuvred the chariot back into the air.

When the chariot was over Madhya Pradesh, Vishwakarma asked Megha if she would like to visit Bhopal for it was alive with a lot of nawabi traditions. Vishwakarma said, "There is a popular saying in Bhopal which goes something like this:

char cheez asth tofa-ay Bhopal
dibbia batua choonaiti rumal"
(There are four treasures of Bhopal—the paanbox, the pouch, the chuna applicator and the kerchief)

Vishwakarma landed his chariot in the outskirts of Bhopal and took Megha to Balwant, a specialist in making paan *dibbas* or boxes. They entered his store where a large number of paan boxes were stacked on the floor. Balwant offered his salutations to Vishwakarma and holding Megha by the hand made her sit on a low stool. Taking

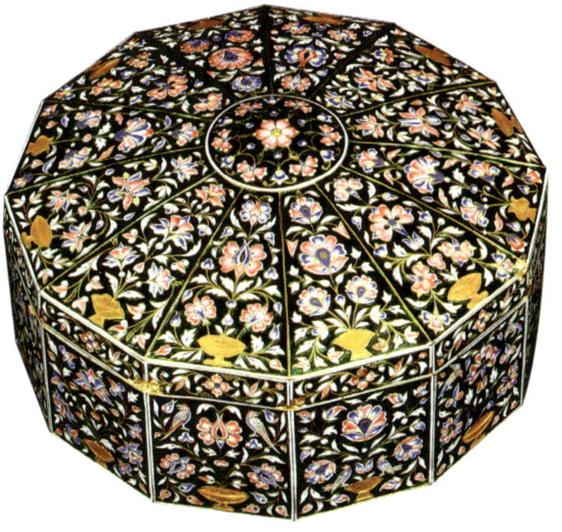

Paan *dibba*, Bhopal

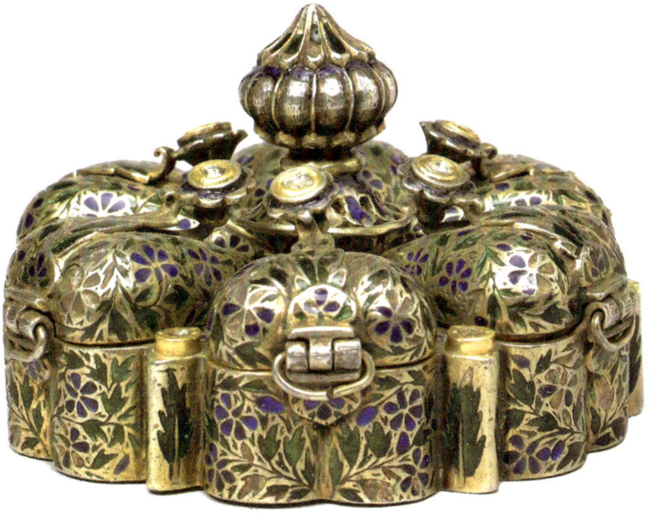

a paan box in his hand he said, "The *dibbia*, *batua*, *choonaiti* and *rumal* are an integral part of the culture of paan in Bhopal. The *dibbia* is an ornately engraved silver box and is used to store paans. The *batua* carries the ingredients like *laung*, *elaichi*, *supari* and zarda. The *choonaiti* is attached to the *batua* with a silver ring and has various implements like a container for *choona*, an assortment of ornate bottles for attar and an ear pick. The *rumal* is used for wrapping the paan and wiping hands." While Megha was admiring the paan box Balwant continued, "The heart of a Bhopali home is the takht with its large bolsters; it is here that friends and family converge and amidst banter and gossip, paan is shared and eaten. The Bhopali *batua* used to be an important part of this ceremony. An offering of the *batua* to another indicated friendship, respect and even love. It was also carried on shikars. *Batuas* were made in different shapes and sizes and of different materials. Velvet, satin or brocade embossed or embroidered ones were popular for special occasions. The Bhopali *batua* is an integral part of the nawabi culture of Bhopal."

Vishwakarma intervened, "A Sanskrit verse extols the virtues of *tambul* or paan in the following lines: *tambulasya sarve trayodasa gunah svargepi durlabaha*—search the heavens and you will not find the many qualities of *tambul*. Mythology has it that Mohini distributed *amrita* amongst the various gods. The urn with the remaining nectar was kept near Indra's elephant Nagaraja. Out of the urn grew the *tambul* creeper and the gods became ecstatic when they ate its leaves. Vishnu ordered Dhanvantari to examine the creeper and it was he who extolled its qualities. From then on Vishnu began presenting its leaves as a gesture of love and affection. According to another legend, after the Pandava's victory at Hastinapur they began craving for *tambul*. A messenger was sent to the underground abode of the serpent queen. The queen, only too happy to oblige, cut the extreme phalange of her little finger and sent it to the Pandavas. The phalange was planted with great ceremony and soon the *tambul* creeper grew out of it."

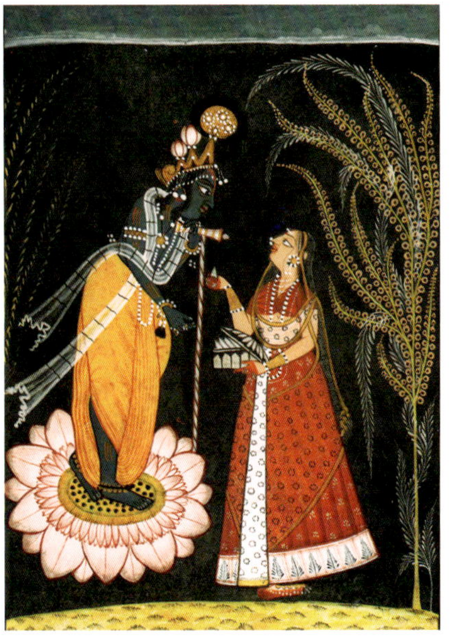

The *tambul* creeper is sometimes also referred to as nagveli. Chosen by the gods and the kings alike, *tambul* is an important part of religious and social ceremonies. No ceremony is complete without the *tambul* leaf. In some marriage ceremonies the bride holds a *tambul* leaf in her mouth and the groom bites it off. Embellished with condiments and chemicals like lime, the *tambul* incorporates many social graces and customs. Between lovers it is a token of affection, in courts it is a sign of friendship and the devout offer it in puja with the words *"pugifalam tambuluam samarpayami"*. The Indian cultural fabric is so intricately woven with the fine threads of religion and mythology that it becomes difficult to determine where a social custom ends and a religious rite begins in day-to-day life. Meshed with this is the colourful *tambul* tradition, which acts as a link between every Indian social relationship.

Vishwakarma's chariot was now crossing the Vindhyas and he related the story of Rishi Agastya to Megha.

"The Deccan is a very special part of India. There have been very few invasions here and the people have been able to maintain the purity and sanctity of Hinduism."

The chariot was now above Ujjain and pointing to a temple Vishwakarma said, "This is the

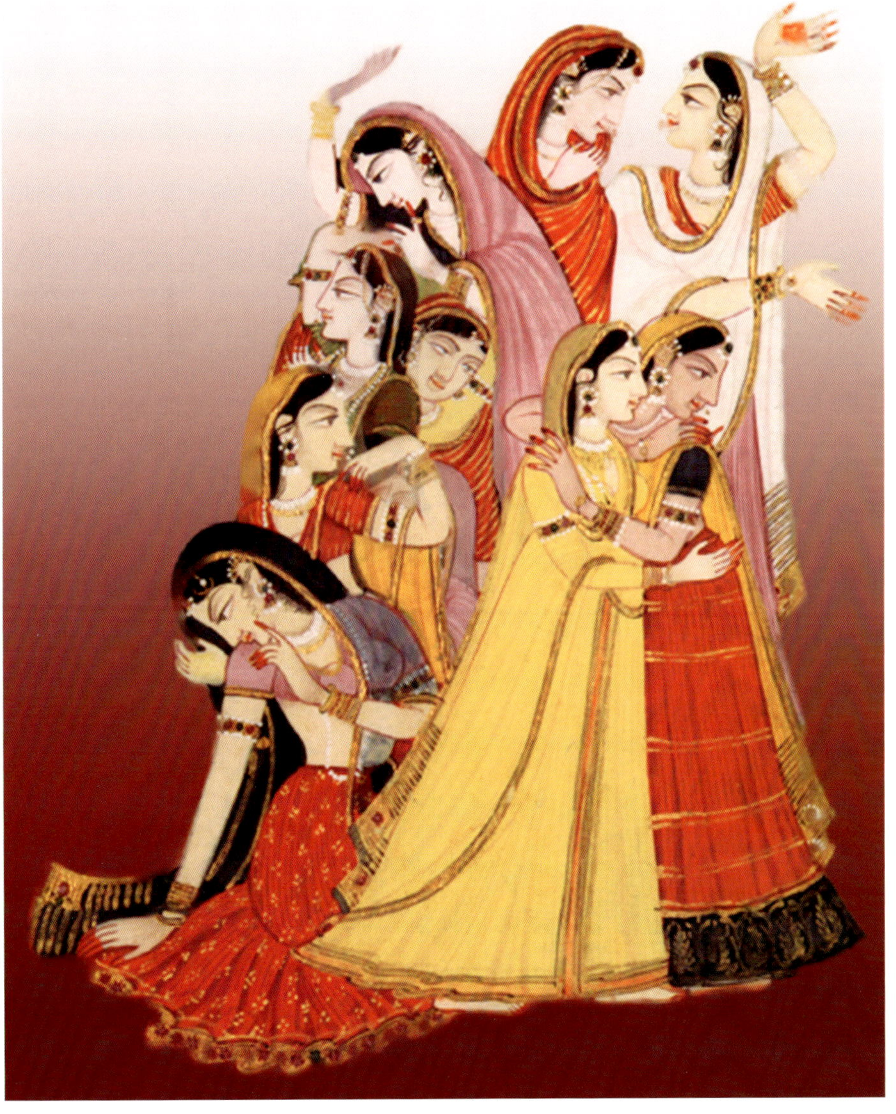

Gopis

Mahakala Temple and it is an important place for Shiva devotees. Also, the noted poet Kalidasa lived here. But today I am taking you to Indore, which was the capital of the Scindias." The chariot descended at a busy marketplace with a number of shops and people milling around. Many of them did not recognise Vishwakarma but bowed to him anyway. He went to a *rangrez* at the end of the street and Megha followed, not quite understanding what was going on. "Let me introduce you to Babulal. He is a *rangrez* and he prepares various colours."

Babulal welcomed them and asked Vishwakarma to sit on a makeshift seat while he took Megha inside. There were a number of pots containing various colours—red, blue and yellow. Babulal said: "Red, blue and yellow are the primary colours and all the rest are created by mixing these." A number of fabrics of different colours were hanging outside his shop. "These are chunnis made on special order for a young lady who is getting married. Did you know that only when a girl comes of age does she begin to wear a red chunni? And a khayal bandish goes like this:

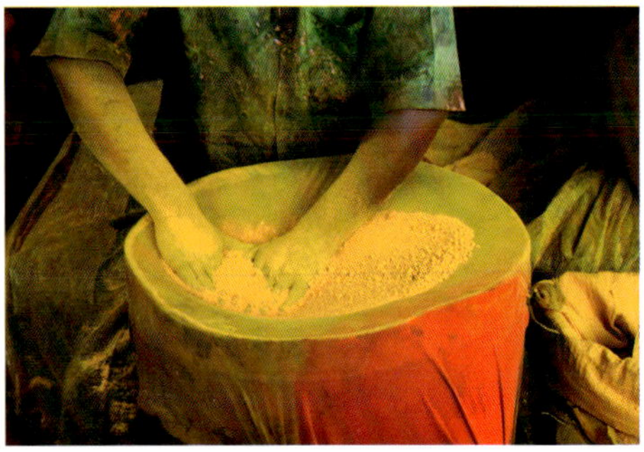

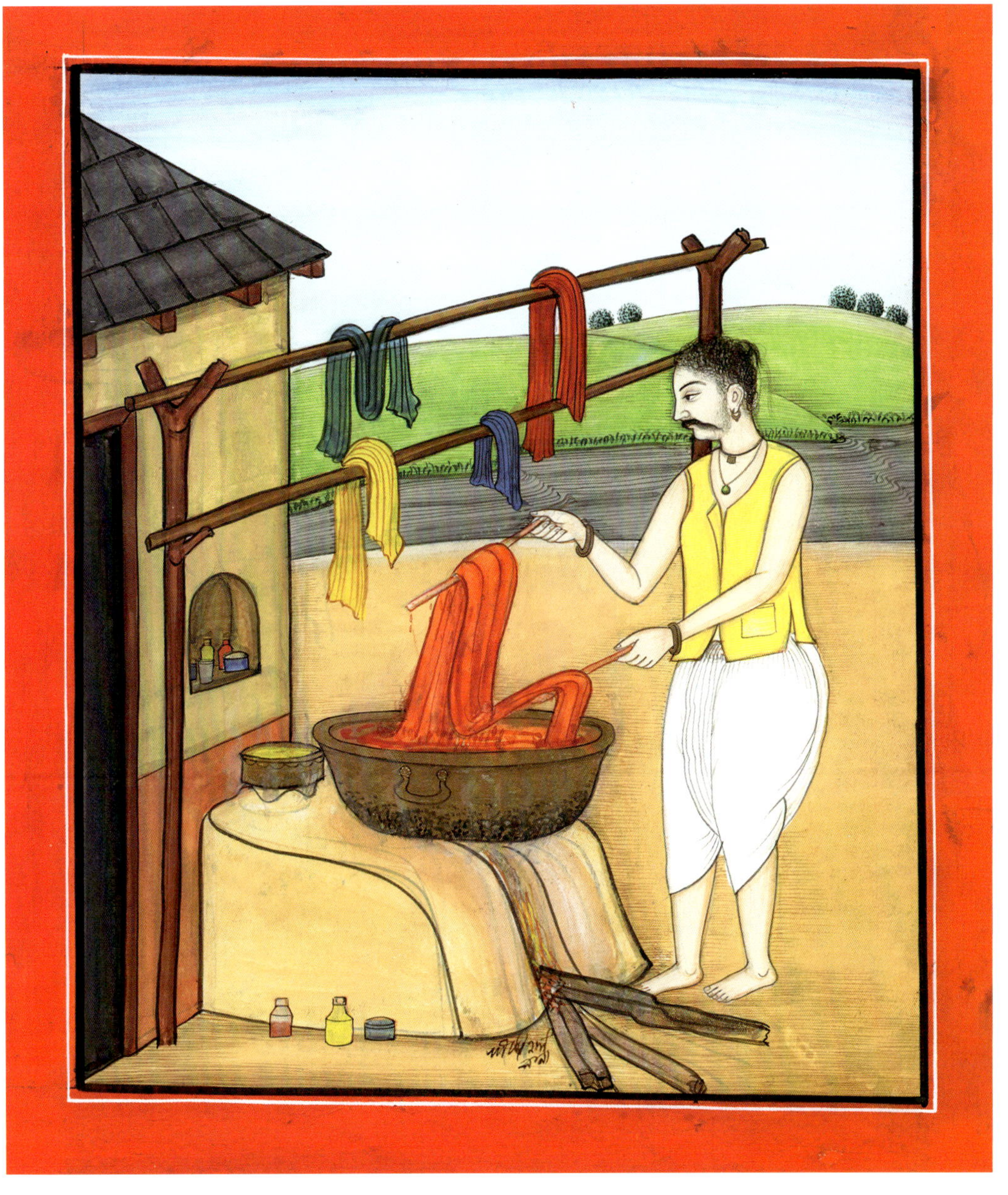

Rangrez, painting by Parikshit Sharma

chunar mori aisi
rangde re rangrejava
jo pike mana bhaye
pili chuniriya pi ko na bhaye
dhani rang bhar de
rangrejava
jo pike mana bhaye
jane piya kon ranga bhaye
sab rang bhara de re
rangrejava
jo pike mana bhaye
(Colour my odhni with colours which please my beloved. He does not like yellow, so make it green O dyer. I really do not know which colour he likes so fill it with all the colours so that my beloved is pleased)

Babulal gave Megha a red-coloured fabric, which she draped around her neck and thought she looked very pretty.

Also sitting in Babulal's shop was Vijay who was a painter of miniatures from Chamba in Himachal. He came close to Megha and said: "The use of colour, boldly yet artistically, was the forte of the Pahari artists. Colours were used not only to capture the landscape but more importantly to convey a distinct mood.

Colours, for us, speak and whisper, sing and dance, and express our moods and feelings better than words. Drawing inspiration from the lush and luxuriant world around—the world of bird and blossom, earth and sky, gems and stones—we use colours not only to beautify and adorn, but equally to create a certain feel. On fabric or canvas, mud wall or floor, sculpture or pots, colours for us have a language, a raga, a rasa and a taal. Red for us denotes passion, yellow young love, blue infinite space and black indicates *viraha* or longing. The use of appropriate colours is particularly seen in Ragamala paintings where the mood of the raga is conveyed as much by colour as by composition. Miniature paintings have rightly been called visual poetry where colour and composition evoke a special mood."

Megha was fascinated. "Tell me more about the different colours." The artist from Chamba said:

"Red is the colour of passion and fertility
of auspiciousness and fecundity,
the colour of the bindi denoting ritual purity
the large dot on the odhani of a young girl
as she comes of age

the radiance of a patola worn at festive occasions
of kumkum that adorns the married woman.

Yellow is the colour of the mango blossoms in chaitra,
of swarms of bees
of intoxicating southern breezes
of sandalwood that is rubbed into paste for rituals, of
pollens of flowers in the spring
the colour of innocence and of romance
of Bengali women during Saraswati puja.

Green is the colour of pallavi
fresh leaves in the spring
the harvest as it ripens in the field, of swaying palms and
verdant fields.

Pink is the colour of Holi
of romantic frivolity between men and women
of tender love and romantic moments.

Black is the colour of kajal, and alluring eyes
of a starless night, and of the abhisarika as she leaves
to meet her beloved.

Rani is the colour of royalty
of regal dignity, of courtly intrigue and splendour.

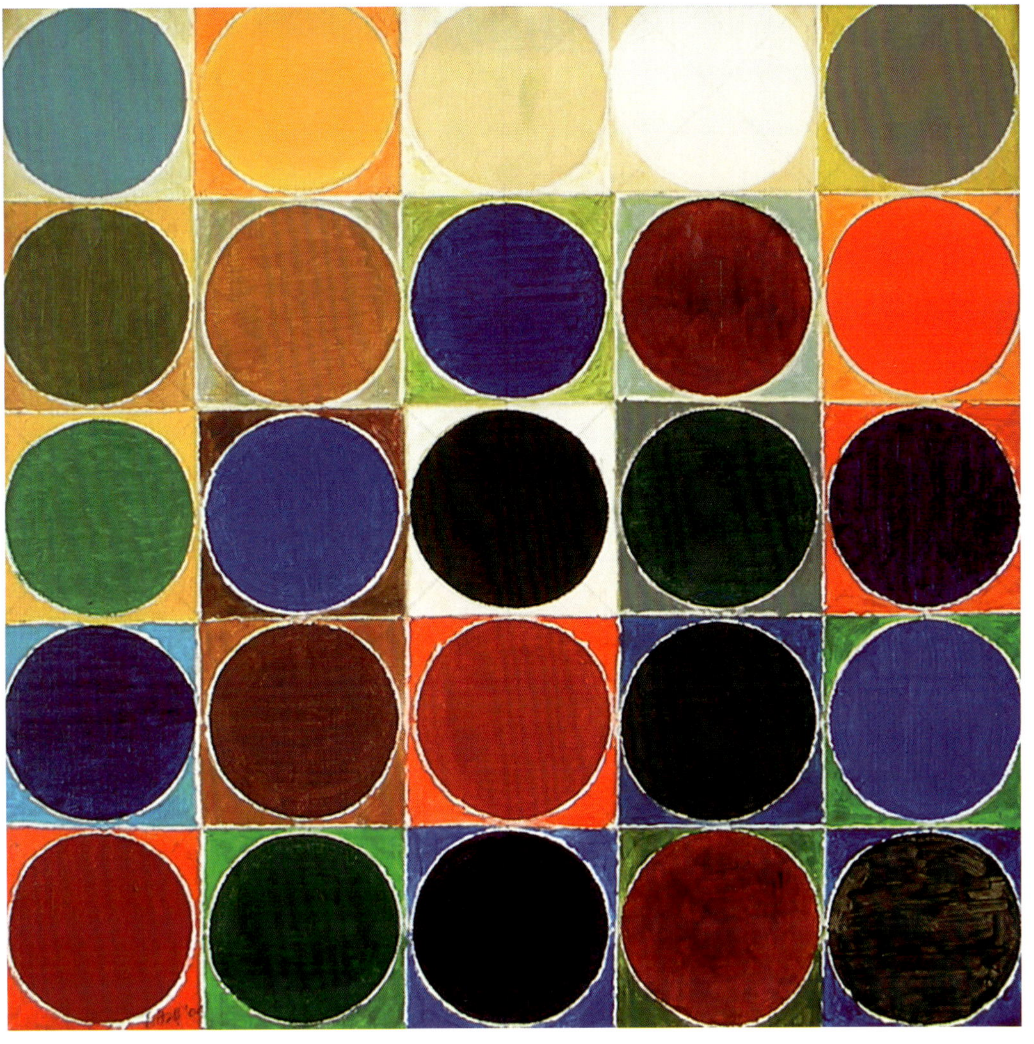

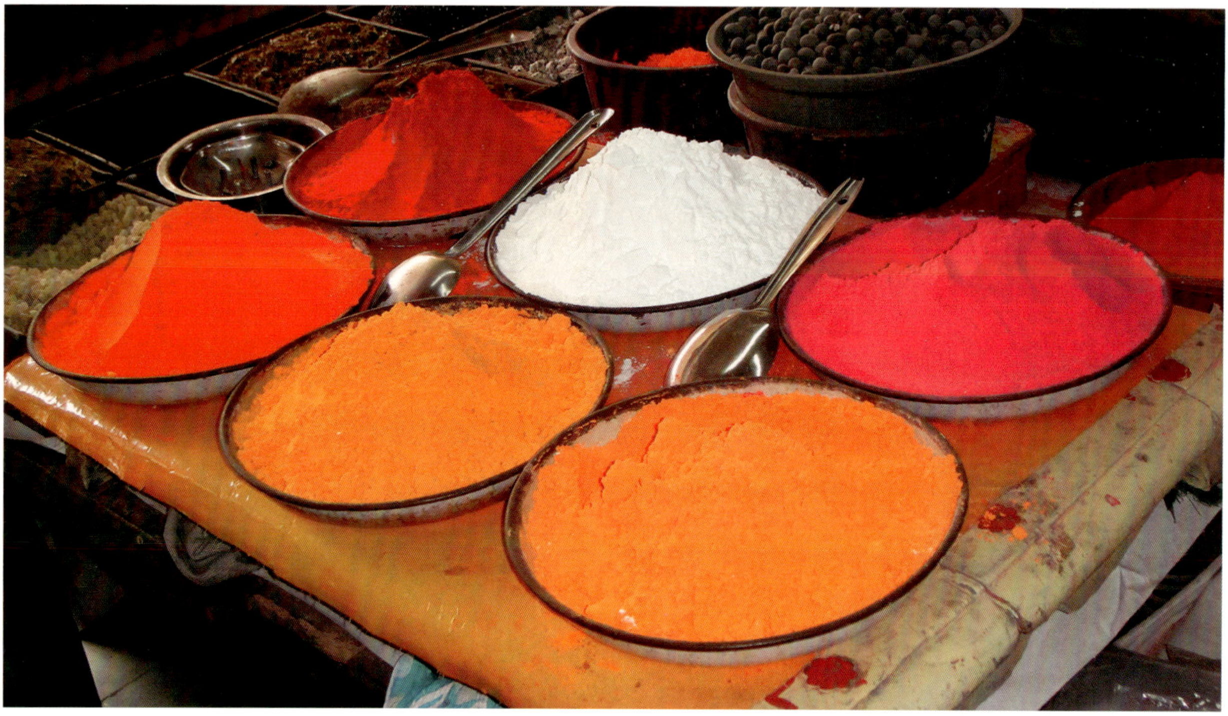

Popati is the colour of the loquacious parrot
of storytelling and languid afternoons.

Mehendi is the colour of coy maidens, as they get ready
for the festivities of a wedding."

Just then a singer with an *ektara* came wandering by singing a bhajan. Vishwakarma blessed him and turning to Megha said:

"In Sanskrit there are two similar words: varna and raga. Varna is the colour of a person or a feature which characterises that person, its psyche and its persona, but varna cannot touch another person. Raga, on the other hand, also means colour but raga resonates and touches and colours the world around it. Our scriptures say that each and every expression of this universe has its own rhythm, its own vibration, its own sound and sweetness and especially its own colour, and thus its own form as well. Vishnu is blue, Shiva has a green neck and Kali is black. Of all the names of Krishna, Ghanashyam is the most evocative for through colours it brings before us the image of Krishna. Blue-black like the clouds of Ashadha, full of nourishing rain, which brings all of Vrindavana

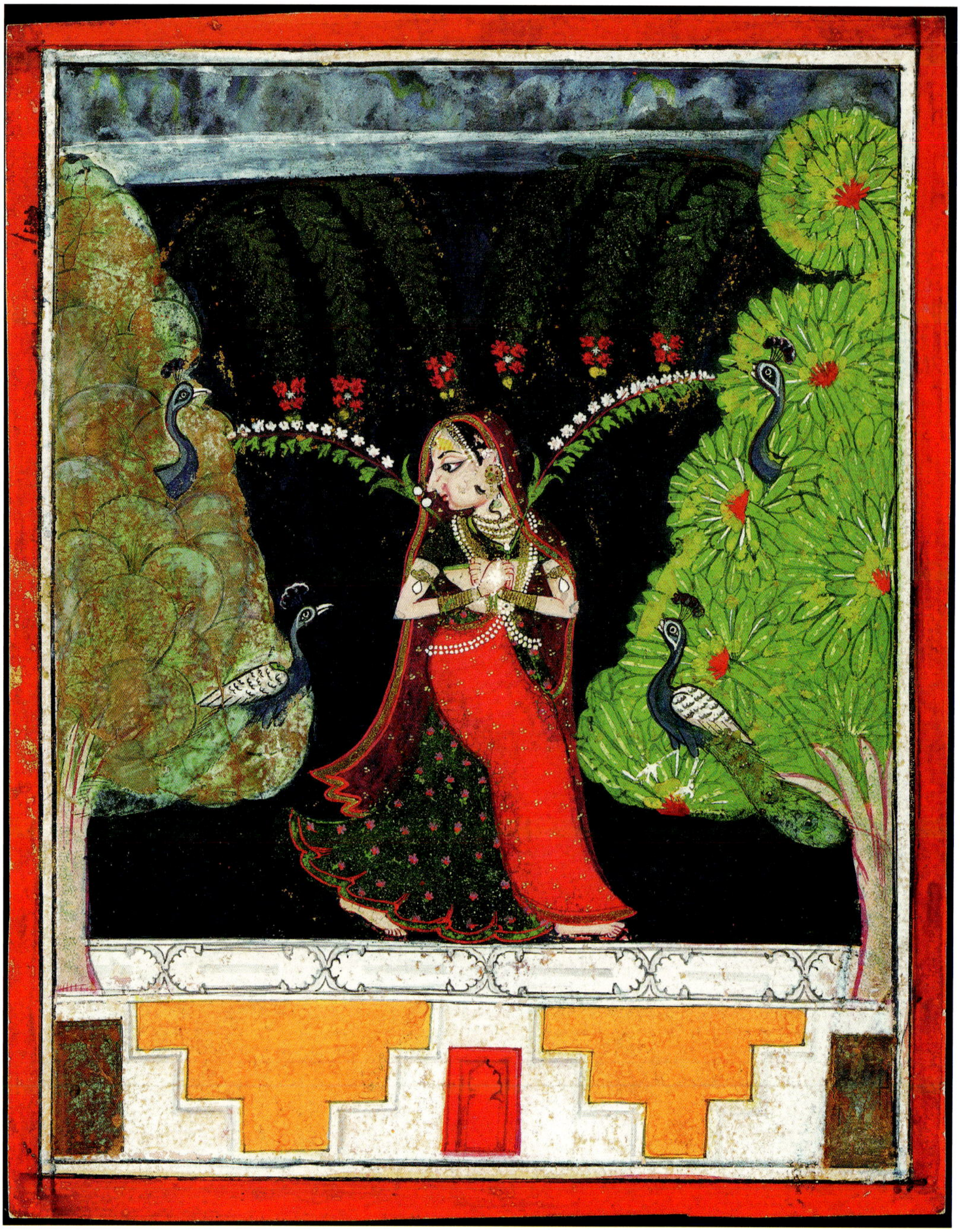

Gauri Ragini, Rajasthan, 18th century

with its luxuriant trees and beautiful blossoms, verdant landscape and limpid waters of the Yamuna, to life. With rain comes the dancing peacock and the songs of the kokila as *gopas* and *gopis* perform the dance of raga Megha Malhar. And through the sound of the word Ghanashyam we begin to hear the flute of Shri Krishna and are transported into another world, a world of *madhurya*, of sweetness, of fond affection and loving togetherness. A world where one loses oneself into another until there is no other, just Krishna playing the flute, which converts time into eternity, Gokula into Goloka and our world into a Vrindavana. All of this through the sound and resonance of the word Ghanashyam."

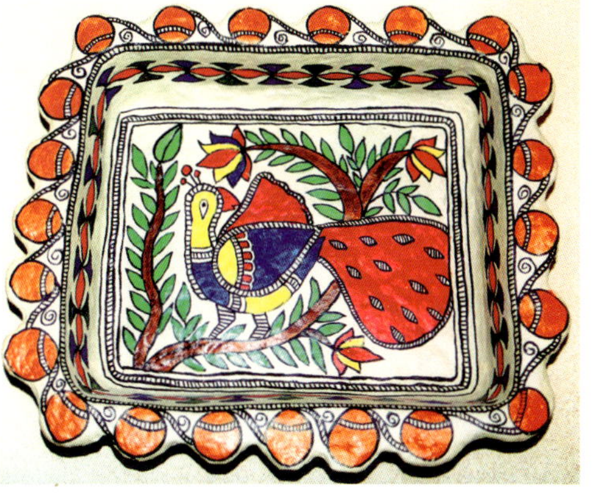

Megha was overwhelmed by everything that she heard about colours. She had never realised how important colours were. As she was preparing to leave, Babulal applied kumkum to her forehead and said, "May you always be happy."

Megha folded her hands and as she walked towards the chariot she thought to herself that she would ask her mother to bring her here when she was getting married to choose the right colour for her.

Next to Madhya Pradesh is the state of Jharkhand. Vishwakarma brought the chariot down in the small village of Hazaribagh in this state. Megha saw little children playing, elderly women sitting on a charpoy and the men drawing on their huqqa sitting under a large Banyan tree. The midday sun was hot and at a distance Megha could see people working on a farm. Close by, pigeons were frolicking and chickens were looking after their young ones. This was a tribal village and there was rustic simplicity all around. In particular, there was something special about the huts—their outer walls were beautifully painted with white patterns. Megha was quite taken by this and just then a young woman came out of a hut and greeted Megha.

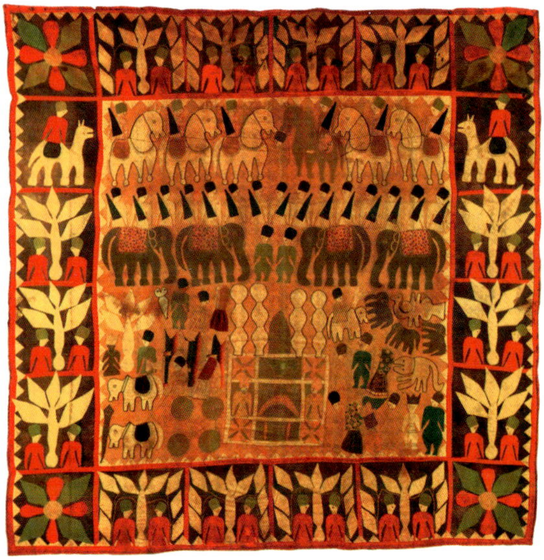

"I am Lakshmi and what is your name?"
"I am Megha." and with those words she folded her hands. "Namaste."

"So, what brings you here today?"
"I have come here with Vishwakarma and am studying the crafts of India."
"Let me then tell you a little bit about our culture. We are adivasis and were the first people of this country. We live in close harmony with nature—the trees and shrubs, birds and blossoms, the chicken and the goats, cows and bulls. Our life is shaped by the seasons, our body by the rhythms of the earth and our mind resonates with the sun and the moon. Rain for us is a blessing and as it falls and nourishes our earth, we dance and sing. We feel most comfortable in these surroundings as our mind is tied to the world of nature. That is why we choose vegetative, rather than geometric or abstract, motifs in the various adornments on our homes. The tree and the creeper, the flower and the blossom, the river and the rain, the sun and the stars—these are our motifs. We are children of this earth and we never forget that bond; we live in harmony with it. To us, our trees are our friends, the animals are our family, the birds are special messengers and the earth our mother. It is in a handful of earth that we hear the footfalls of our ancestors whom we worship and their spirit guards us. Our home is our

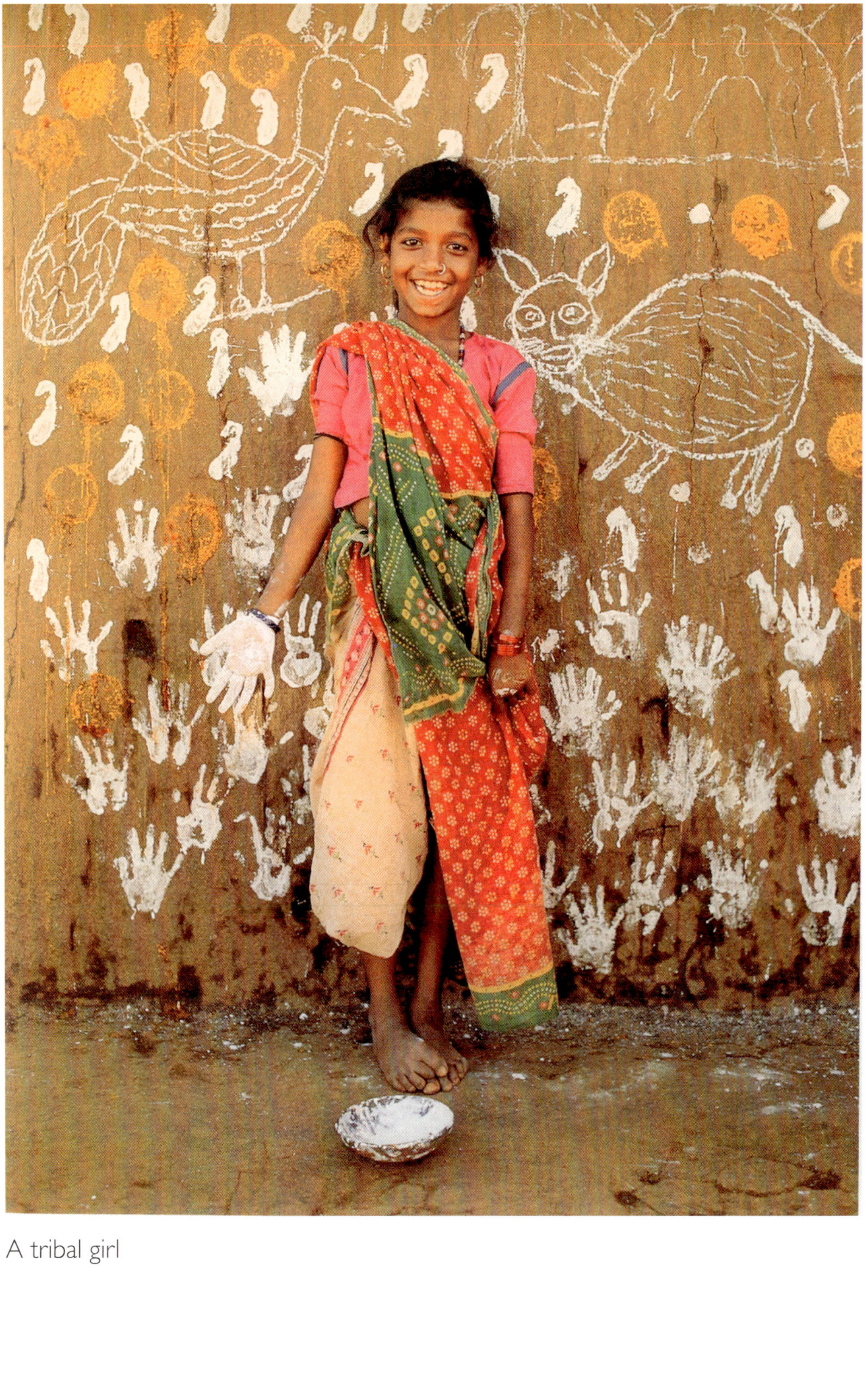

A tribal girl

refuge and we adorn it and beautify the walls with rice paste."

Lakshmi took Megha to her home. A heap of cow dung was kept in a corner with some white paste in a container. Lakshmi took a small stick to which was attached a piece of cloth and dipping it in the rice paste she began to make patterns on a wall that was prepared with cow dung. She drew a tree and painted a *kalash* underneath it. Above the tree she made the sun and placed two birds on the branches of the tree.

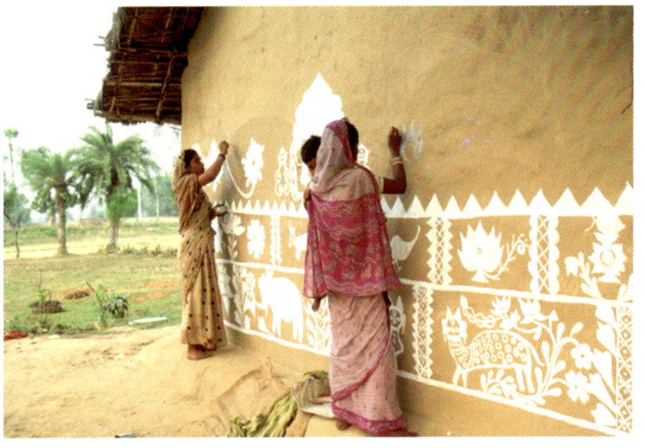

Megha watched in silent admiration. Lakshmi then handed her a brush with which Megha drew a lotus.

"That is very beautiful," Lakshmi said, "but you will have to come back next year and paint it again for we wipe away these patterns and make new adornments each year. In particular, we will never leave our door bare for it is what separates the comfort and security of our home from the chaos and the uncertainty of the world outside. It is at the door that we receive our guests and it is here that we bid them goodbye when they go out for the commerce of the day. Doors are very special for us." Megha was pleased and thanked everyone and Lakshmi gave her a little bit of the rice paste to take home with her. "There is a certain magic in the rice paste and we do not use paint from a tube for that would be too synthetic. The motifs and designs that we make using rice paste protect us and our homes."

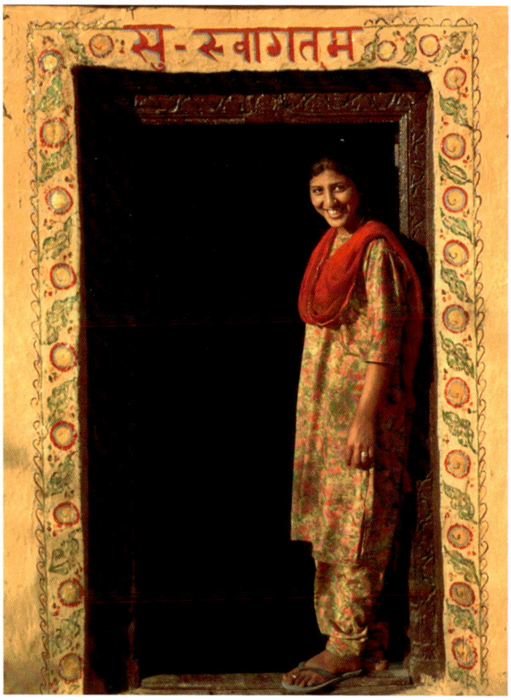

The chariot was flying over Maharashtra and Vishwakarma told Megha that this was the land of bhakti poets like Tukaram and Eknath. He kept on talking about the whole bhakti movement when the chariot landed in a small town on the Godavari River.

"This is Paithan, where Eknath lived," he said and spotting him Baji Rao, dressed in a dhoti, came and prostrated himself.

"What brings you to our humble home?"

"I want you to meet my young friend Megha who wants to learn about your craft," Vishwakarma said blessing Baji Rao.

Holding Megha by the hand Baji Rao took her inside his house where there were two looms and a number of people working on them.

"Paithan is the home of a traditional fabric which is prized all over India and especially in Maharashtra—the Paithani sari. It is believed that the art and craft of weaving Paithani saris goes back to the Satavahana kingdom. It is woven with gold and silver threads and the motifs are drawn from the world around us, especially from the murals of Ajanta. It takes anywhere from six to nine months to complete one sari. Our saris have traditional colours and their distinguishing feature is the beautiful *pallu*. The trousseau of a Maharashtrian bride is incomplete without a Paithani sari. This fabric is the pride of our state. Come to Paithan when you get married and we will gladly give you one of our saris."

Megha went and stood beside a loom and touched the various threads. She was quite moved by the kindness of Baji Rao.
Baji Rao took out a sari that was ready and unrolled it to show the *pallu*. Indicating the various motifs he said, "This is the Ajanta lotus and this the *aam butta* or the mango motif. Look

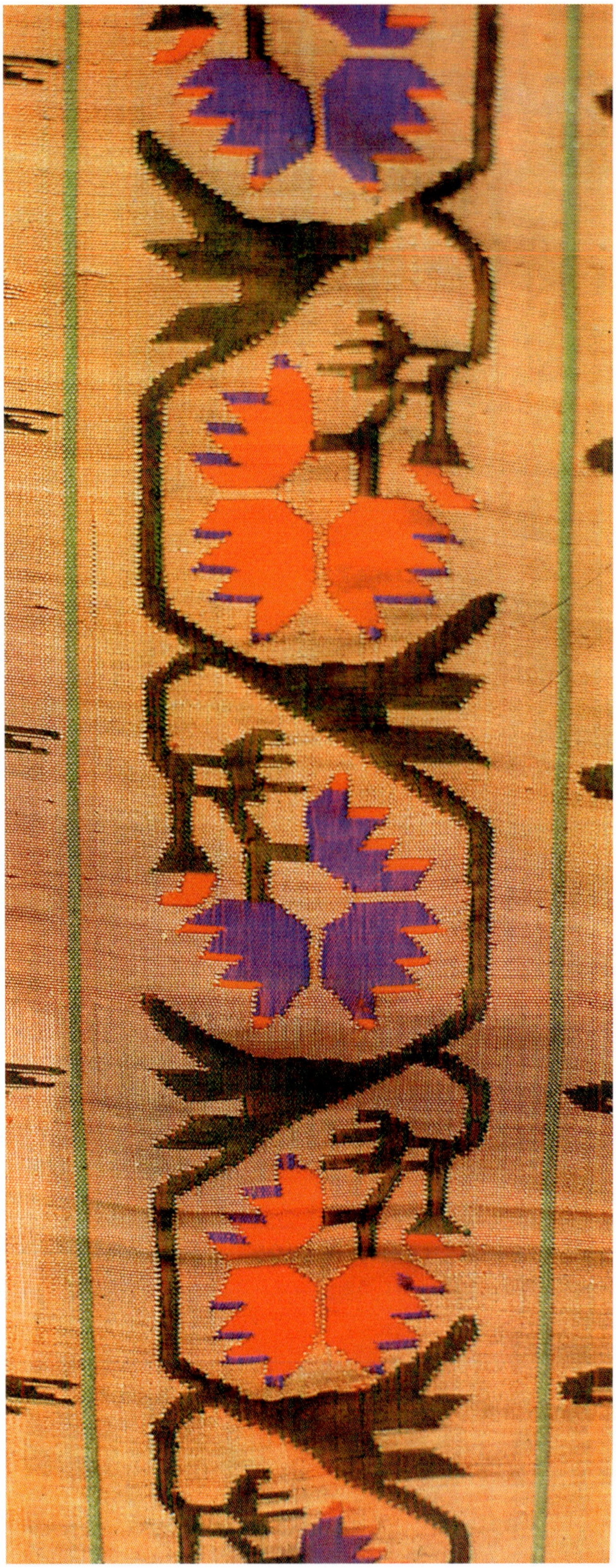

our family for the last hundred years," Vishwas said. He gave her a small copper loti. Megha thanked him and went back to the chariot. Back in the chariot she showed the loti to Vishwakarma and he told her that of all the pots in our country the lota and the *ghada* or the *kalash* were the most important.

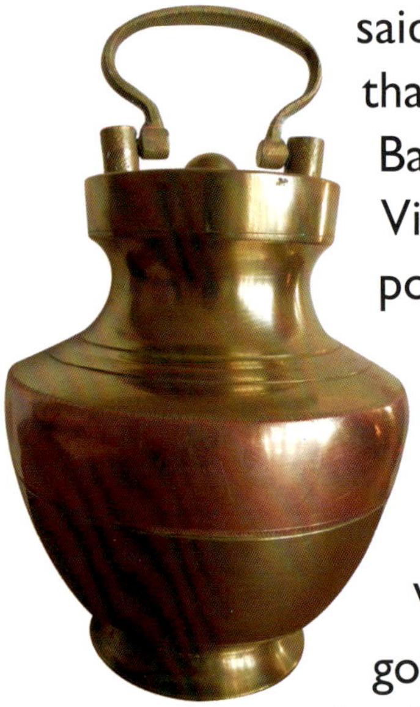

The chariot was now flying over Ahmedabad in the state of Gujarat and Vishwakarma told Megha that he was going to take her to Patan to see a very rare kind of fabric. The chariot landed in Patan and Vishwakarma and Megha walked to the home of Narottamdas.

He was working on a loom and seeing them he got up and received them with great respect.
"Salutations to you guruji, what brings you to our home today?"
"I want you to show how you make the Patola to my young friend Megha."
"Meghaben, *swagat*," so saying Narottamdas took Megha to the loom where his brother was working. "We are the only family that makes this rare and prized fabric of Gujarat."
"Please tell me more about it," Megha said.

"Patola is a celebrated fabric from Gujarat and claims its ancestry to the tenth century. It is believed that a group of women from Andhra Pradesh migrated to Patan and started a unique weaving process, which was to later become the Patola. These migrants were Jains and got the patronage of Siddharaja Jayasingh's mother who encouraged them to create the exquisite Patola in Patan. The Patola belongs to the generic group of ikat but has a richer weave and more intricate design and over the centuries has become the most treasured fabric for a Gujarati bride. The fabric features animal motifs like the elephant, flowers like the lotus and even geometrical designs.

"The fame of the Patola has spread beyond Gujarat. Centuries ago it was exported to Malaysia and Indonesia and was bartered by traders in Arabia and China. In the fifteenth century, European traders came to India to buy the Patola. In Andhra Pradesh the Patola is used even today as a temple hanging and in Kerala it is wrapped around idols. Weavers and wearers ascribe magical properties to the Patola and it is said that although the fabric will tear, the colours will never fade. Though it's not a religious fabric

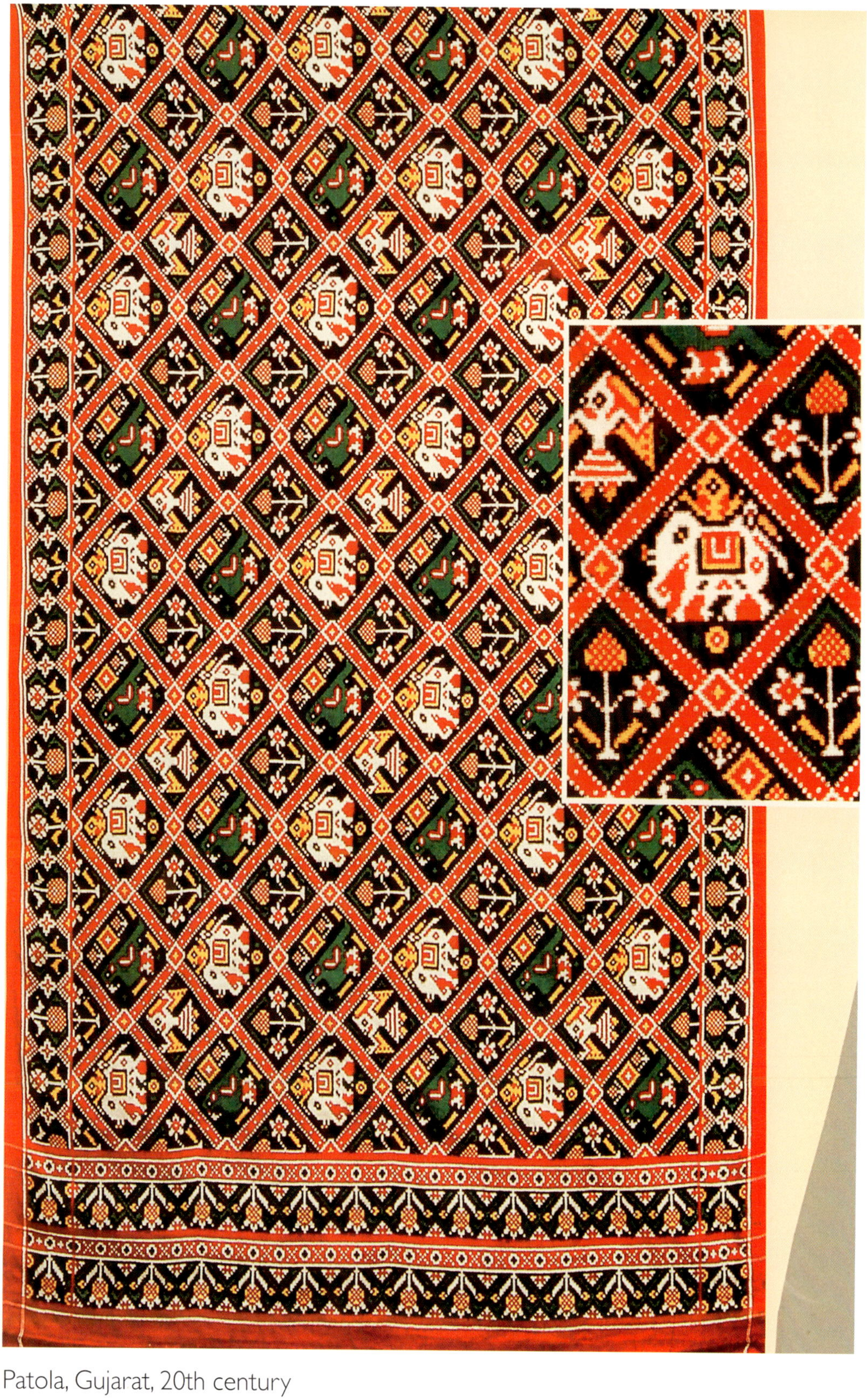

Patola, Gujarat, 20th century

it gives a certain sanctity to the Gujarati bride. It has rightly been said that the weaving of the Patola is a dream and a prayer."

Vishwakarma rose and bringing them together said:

"The relationship between an Indian woman and fabric is very special. At every event and circumstance, festival or celebration, she not only imparts her beauty to the fabric but makes the fabric come alive. Colour and texture, design and motif, *rachana* and *akriti*, become animated with her touch. She knows infinite ways in which a simple fabric can be transformed into a multidimensional art object. The manner in which the cloth is draped, the way it cascades, the new folds created with each bodily movement, the way the *pallu* dances with each step that she takes, how keys that are tied to its end chime, the changes in texture and colour with every step or shade of light constantly shows the beauty of the fabric to the sensitive eye and a romantic heart. Someday when you get older you must collect saris from every part of India and wear them with a flourish and joyous abandon!"

Megha was fascinated by the story of Patola and

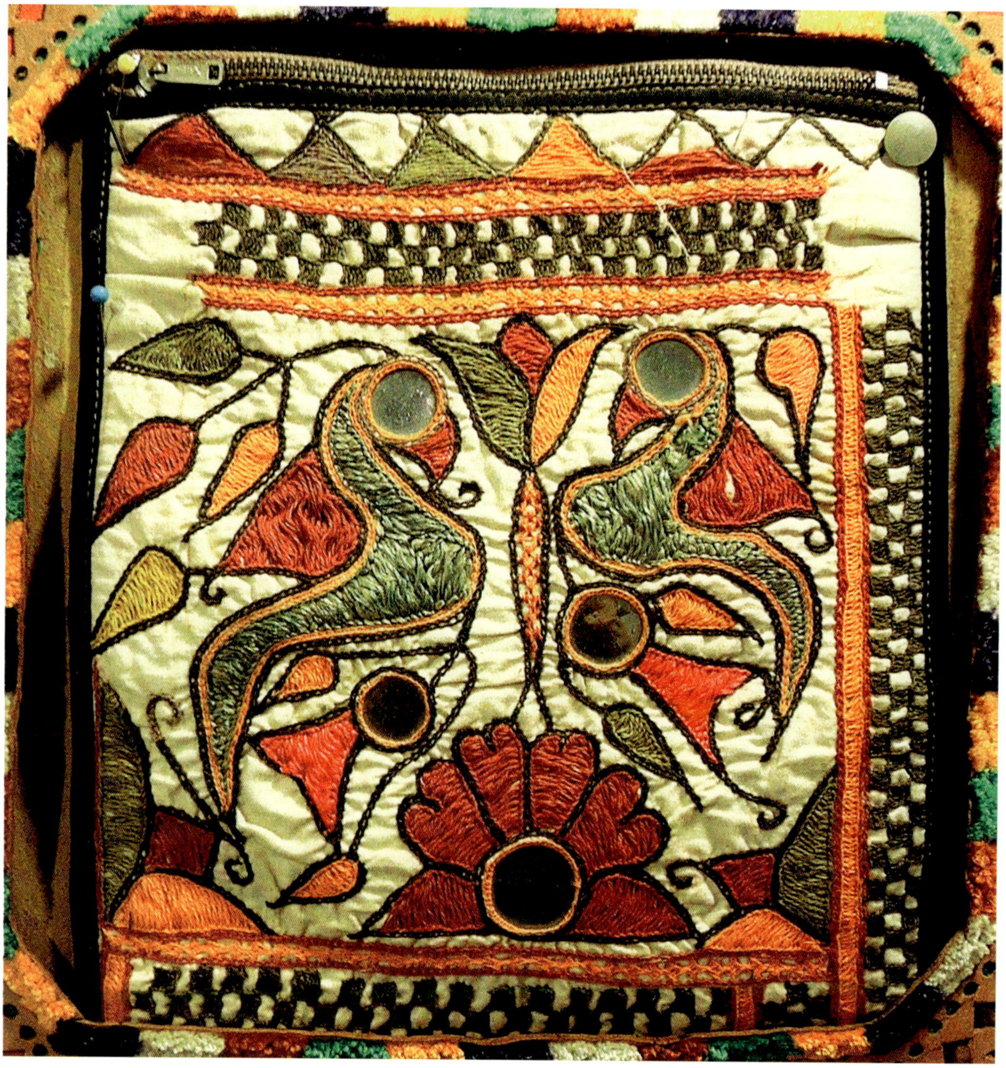

the beauty of a sari and she spent a long time looking over the loom. Narottamdas's brother gave her a few threads which she tied around her wrist and after bidding them farewell turned towards the chariot.

Before leaving Gujarat, Vishwakarma spoke to Megha about another fabric that is important to the Gujaratis. Holding Megha by the hand as they walked towards the chariot he said, "A fabric very special to Gujarat is the chandarvo. For Gujaratis the chandarvo, a richly embroidered fabric, is the mother goddess herself and its real purpose is as an offering at a shrine of the goddess.

"The Gujarati weaver, when finished making the chandarvo, dances and sings and goes into a trance. At the moment of his trance the weaver drapes the chandarvo around him to establish identity with the goddess. Anyone, it is said, can make a chandarvo but only a bhakta of the mother can breathe life into it. Another fabric of religious significance to the Gujaratis is the mata-ni-pachedi, which is a fabric on which images of the goddess are painted or printed and used to make a sacred enclosure for the celebration of the goddess."

at the *mor* or peacock, *tota-maina* or the parrots, *asawalli* or flowering vines and *humarparinda* or peasant bird."

Megha thanked everyone at Baji Rao's home and as she was preparing to leave, his wife applied kumkum to her forehead and said "*Parat laukar ye*"—come back soon.

Vishwakarma said that he wanted to visit another sacred city on the Godavari and that was Nashik. He landed the chariot on the banks of the river where a number of people were performing rituals. "Come and meet Vishwas," he said.

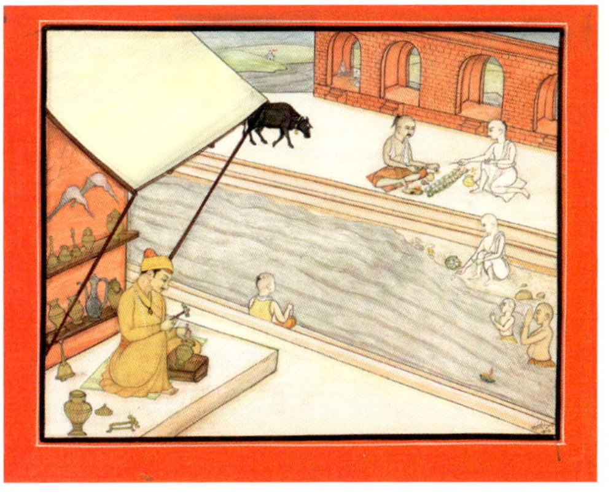

Vishwas had a shop right on the banks of the Godavari and he made and sold a variety of metal lotas and pots. When Megha went there he greeted her and showed her the many different lotas. One in particular, he said, was very beautiful, which he called the Ganga-Jamuni lota. It was made of brass and copper and people bought it to take home the waters of the Godavari as it is considered the Ganga of the south. "We have been doing this in

"We cannot leave Gujarat without visiting the Rabaris of Kutch," Vishwakarma said.

"Who are Rabaris?" Megha asked.

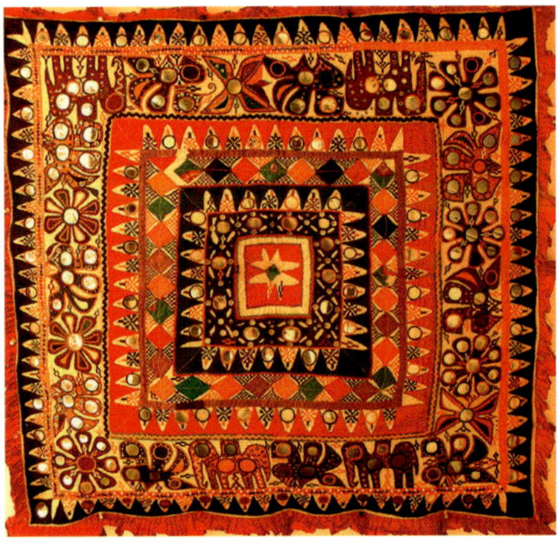

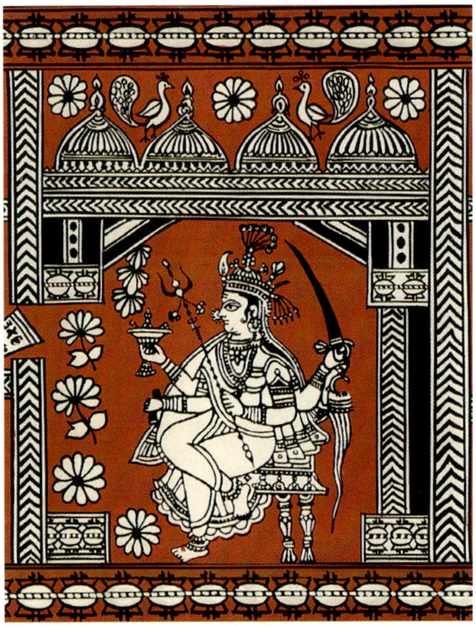

Steering the chariot towards Kutch Vishwakarma said, "They are camel herders and lead an itinerant lifestyle." As he spoke he landed the chariot in a sandy desert. There were small circular homes called *bhongo* all around and in the midday sun camels were resting under a thorny tree. Nearby, women wearing colourful clothes and a lot of ivory bangles were embroidering multicoloured fabrics.

Seeing Vishwakarma the men got up and welcomed him and he in turn introduced Megha to them.

The women befriended Megha and soon they were chatting and she was learning all about the different stitches. She was quite taken by all the colours and patterns of Kutchi embroidery and even tried a few stitches herself. She asked the women why they wore such large ivory bangles and she was told that this was their savings bank. If they ever needed money they could sell their bangles for they would fetch good money. She particularly liked the *kothlo* or a bag with embroidery and decided that she was going to buy it to take her lunch to school. This was Megha's first exposure to the adivasis of India, the first settlers. She wondered how ancient their civilisation was and what India was like in those hoary days. Megha was not only learning about the various objects that the craftspeople made but the many sides to the tradition, its history and sociology, its art and aesthetics. Craft no longer remained just an object of utility but became for her an object of art.

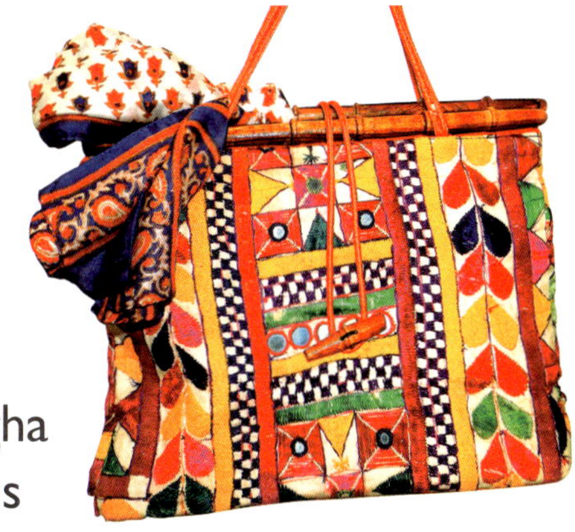

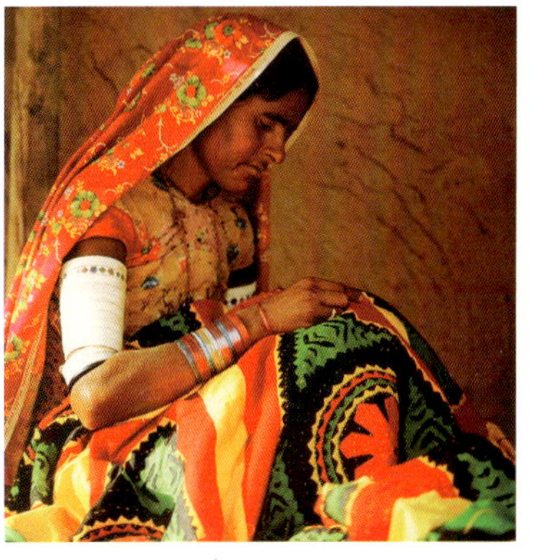

Vishwakarma would take time to explain to Megha the finer points of Indian traditions for he felt that one cannot enjoy crafts in isolation. They must be understood in totality with life and living. He said, "Did you know that we in India preferred terracotta over ceramics? Terracotta cups for instance were used only once and then discarded but ceramic was used over and over again and therefore considered polluted. Ceramic came to India from China and ceramic tiles were Persian." Just as he was speaking the chariot reached Jaipur and Vishwakarma decided to show Megha the crafts and traditions of the city. Even from the sky Megha could see the familiar sights of Jaipur—the Hawa Mahal, Jantar Mantar and Govinddevji Temple; the pink city looked so beautiful. No sooner did they land, Vishwakarma took Megha by the hand and walked towards the home of Hukam Singh who was a potter. In his backyard was a large potter's wheel, a mound of clay, vats of colour and a kiln. Hukam Singh paid his respects to Vishwakarma by touching his feet and welcomed Megha by placing his hand on her head.

"I have brought my young friend to let her see how you make Jaipur blue pottery."
"It will be my pleasure to show it to her. But before I do that let me ask my elder brother Natthuram to give her a short lesson on its history."

Sporting a *pheta* Natthuram, who was dressed in a dhoti, took Megha by the hand and sat on a wooden bench.

"The technique of applying the colour blue on textiles was prevalent in ancient India and we derived this colour from the indigo plant. Indigo vats are to be found in the recovered artefacts of the Indus Valley civilisation. There is also some evidence that in the Buddhist period, blue enamelled tiles were made in India. However, during the classical Gupta period there is no evidence of blue pottery in India. Glazed blue tiles first started appearing in India during the Tughlaq period in the fourteenth century. These were probably brought to India from Turkey or Persia by the many craftsmen who migrated here to escape Mongol persecution.

"Blue tiles were also brought from China where the technology of making blue ceramics was well developed. By the beginning of the fourteenth century, China had mastered the art of high-fired translucent porcelain with brilliantly coloured cobalt-blue paintings. The Mongol Yuan Dynasty of China was closely related to the more westerly Mongols of central Asia and it was this link, created through invasions, that gave China access to Persian cobalt blue. After his pillage of Delhi in the December of 1398, Timur took stonemasons from Delhi to Samarkand and they were the ones responsible for creating his magnificent tomb, the Gur-e Amir. Its beautiful turquoise dome, Persian in inspiration, can be seen as a foretaste of splendours to come. The Persians were experimenting with the use of cobalt blue but it was only in the sixteenth and seventeenth centuries under the Safavids that the technique was perfected."

Megha was listening intently.

Natthuram continued, "In the absence of concrete evidence it would be hazardous to venture a precise date for the beginning of blue pottery in India. But evidence suggests that glazed tile-making preceded blue pottery. Glazed blue tiles are to be seen in the Gwalior fort, built by Raja Man Singh who ruled from 1486 to 1516. The Sheesh Gumbad of the Lodi Gardens was richly decorated with blue tiles. The gateways of Sher Shah Suri's Purana Qila in Delhi, the Jahangir Mahal at Orchha, the outer gateway to the Humayun's tomb and the Rang Mahal at Amber, among others, have blue tiles. The blue tilework was called *kashani* after Kashan in Persia. The use of blue glazed tiles continued through the Mughal period and centres for making such tiles

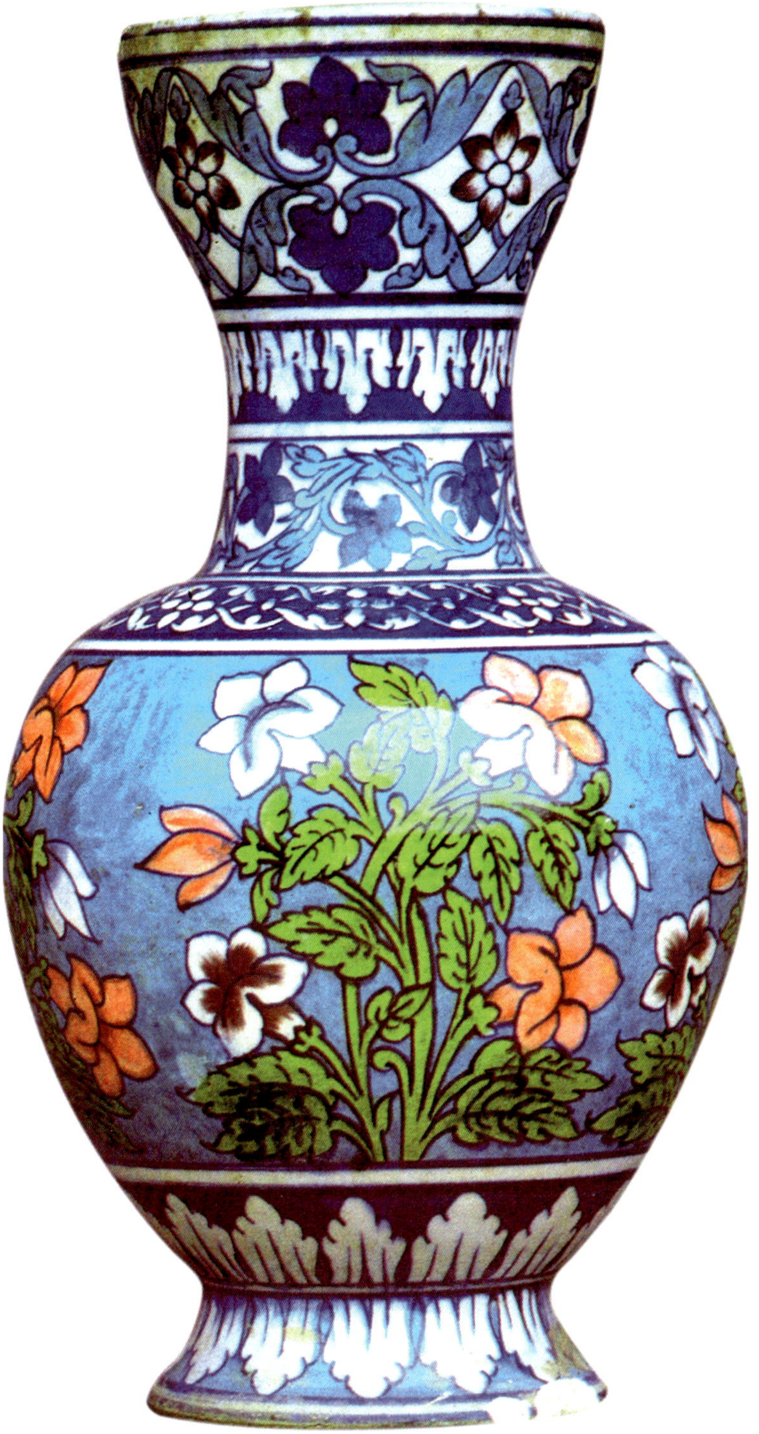

A flower vase in Jaipur blue pottery

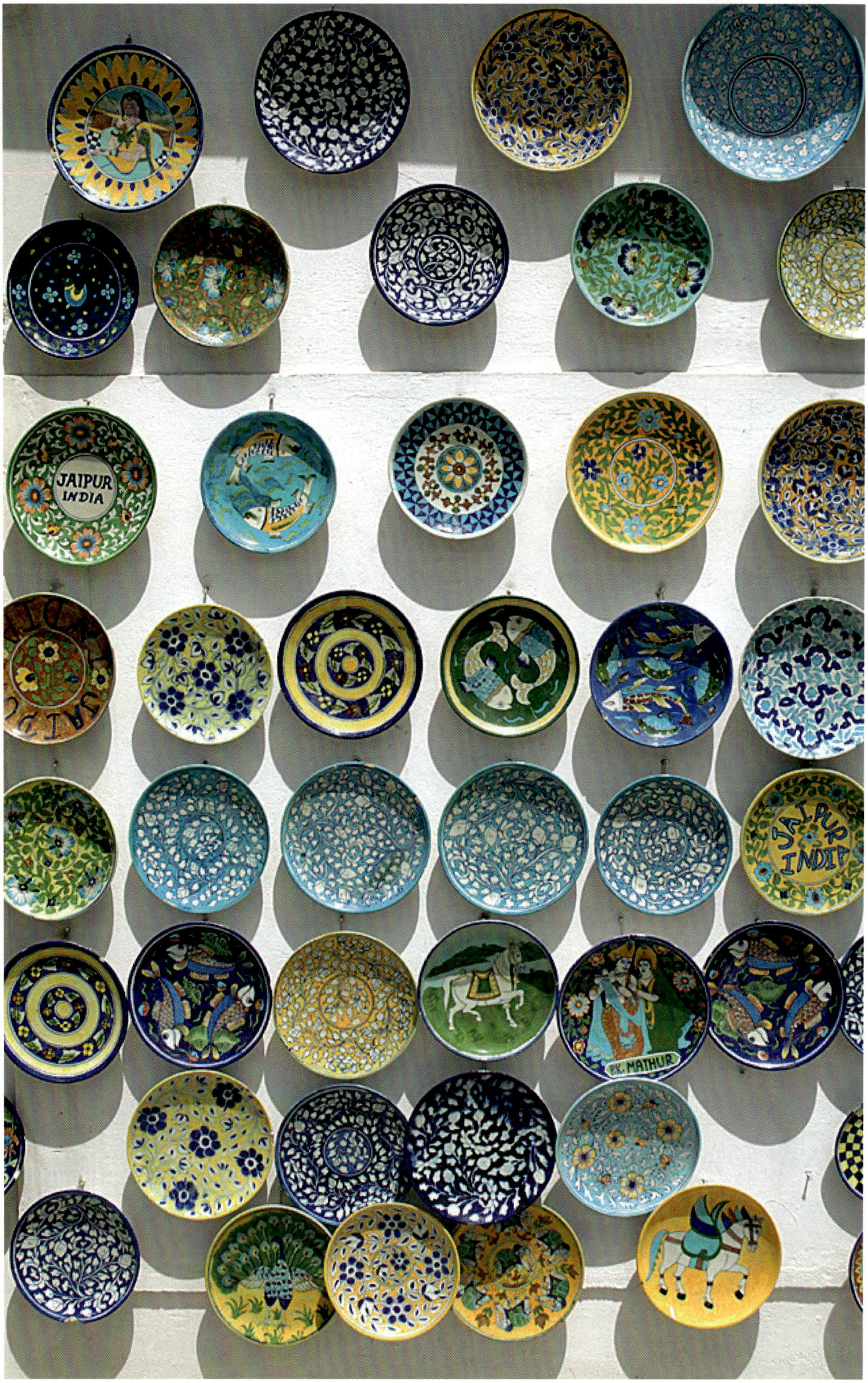

Jaipur blue pottery

were set up in Delhi, Agra, Meerut and Rampur. Having mastered the art of producing glazed tiles, the transition from tiles to pottery was an easy one. Paintings from the *Baburnama* show Babur being served food in blue and white plates. Blue pottery is also seen in paintings in niches of palaces."

Vishwakarma, who was sitting on a low seat under a tree, looked approvingly at Megha.

"When Sawai Jai Singh founded the city of Jaipur in 1727, a number of artisans and craftsmen came from various centres and this included masters of blue pottery. However, it was during the reign of Maharaja Sawai Ram Singh II (r. 1835–1880) in the nineteenth century that blue pottery was patronised by the kings. A story is told of a kite-flying festival when the royal kite was cut by two bothers Churamani and Kaluram who were masters of blue pottery. When the king asked to meet these brothers he learnt that they had coated the kite string with glass dust used in their blue pottery. The king was impressed and asked the brothers to settle down in Jaipur and head the pottery section of the School of Arts, founded in 1866. This was the beginning of the tradition and

Jaipur became a flourishing centre of blue pottery. Sawai Ram Singh also sent the two brothers to Delhi to improve their technique of blue pottery from one Bhola who worked at the court of Emperor Bahadur Shah II (r. 1837–1858).

"The workshops at Jaipur produced vases, water pots, plates and bowls. The motifs on blue pottery are usually floral or geometrical

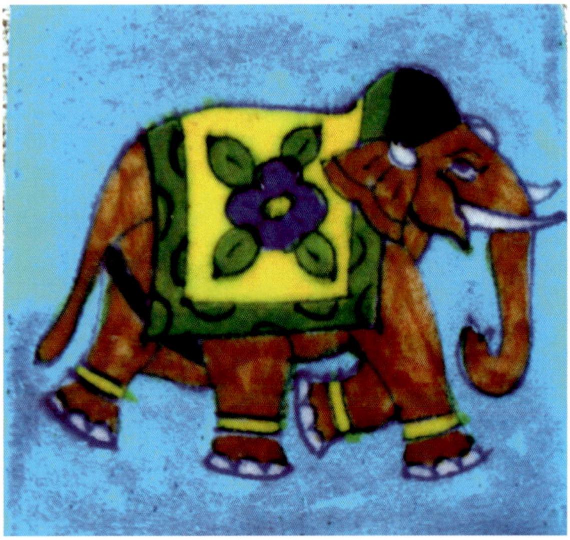

but Rajasthani folk heroes and heroines were also depicted. Jaipur blue pottery is an important part of the craft treasures of India. In Jaipur, the two brothers were given a home in the Goonga Behra ki Gali of Gangori bazaar. They along with their sons produced a number of different pottery items. Two of the finest examples of Jaipur blue, commissioned by Sawai Man Singh II who reigned from 1922 to 1949, are the Polo Bar fountain and Maharani's dressing room at the Rambagh Palace."

Megha was most interested in this history lesson and after Natthuram finished she went with

Hukam Singh to see their studio. She picked up a small broken piece of pottery after taking their permission and thanked everyone for their hospitality. Hukam Singh insisted that they have some food with them but Vishwakarma intervened saying that they had to make another call in Jaipur and took their leave.

Once at their destination Megha and Vishwakarma left the chariot and walked to Jhaveri Bazaar in Jaipur. Vishwakarma took her to a jewellery shop there. Seeing him enter the shop everyone got up and venerated him and Vishwakarma in turn acknowledged their greetings. He then called Rajeshwar, who was an expert jeweller, and asked him to explain to Megha the art of minakari. Rajeshwar took Megha behind the shop, made her sit on a large *dari* and said:

"Minakari or enamelling is the art of painting, colouring and ornamenting the surface of metals by fusing over them brilliant colours in beautiful patterns. The word *mina* is the feminine form of the Persian word *minoo*, which means heaven, and minakari therefore means divine art. The art of minakari originated in Persia and it came to India with the Mughals. The royalty of Jaipur, which was very close to Akbar, brought minakari craftsmen to Jaipur and the art has thrived since then. Minakars belong to the Sonar caste of Kshatriyas and the art has passed on from father to son. Minakari is a complex process in which a single piece of jewellery passes through many expert hands before being completed.

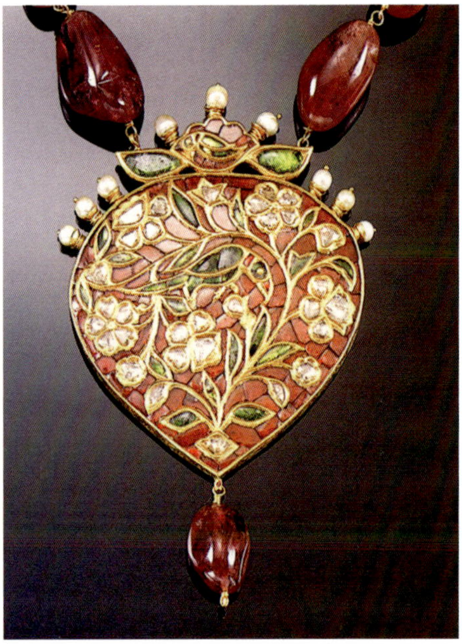

"The traditional process starts with the designer or *nacquash* and moves on to the goldsmith or *sonar*, the kalamkar who engraves the design, the enamellist or minakar who applies the colour, the polisher or *ghotnawala*, the stone-setter or *kundansaaz* and the stringer or *patua*, all of whom are part of an important chain of craftsmen that create the finished product. In Lucknow, the specialty of the minakars was blue and green enamelling on silver, while in Banaras the dusky rose-pink or the *gulabi mina* is the dominant colour. Creepers and vines, flowers—particularly the lotus, birds—especially the parrot and the peacock, paisleys, geometric

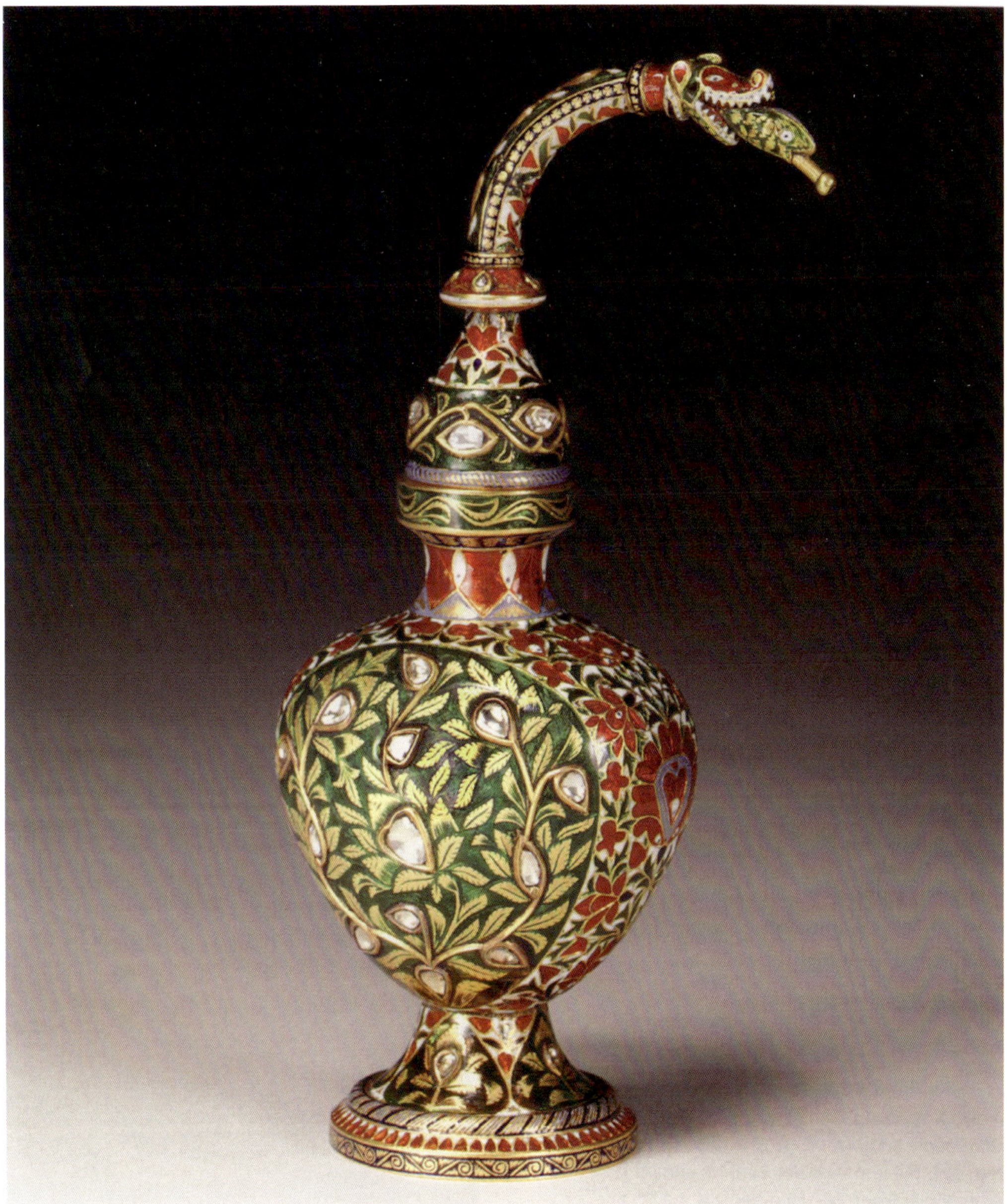

Minakari *huqqa*

patterns and calligraphy are some of the more commonly used designs. The colours used are red, green, white and blue. Minakari is not just confined to traditional jewellery but diversifies into more modern products, often with a copper base, including bowls, ashtrays, keychains, vases, spoons, figures of deities, and wall pieces."

"Can I see some minakari jewellery?" Megha's interest had peaked after hearing the history and technique of minakari jewellery. Rajeshwar brought out a large box containing jewellery. He even placed a pendant around Megha's neck and she admired herself in the mirror but then quickly returned it.

"No, that is for you. It looks just perfect on you." Rajeshwar said. Megha looked at Vishwakarma and only when he nodded did she accept.

There were other people in the jewellery shop and one of them remarked, "Jewellery is only for feminine vanity."

Vishwakarma heard that and said, "No, that is not correct. The human body is the temple of god

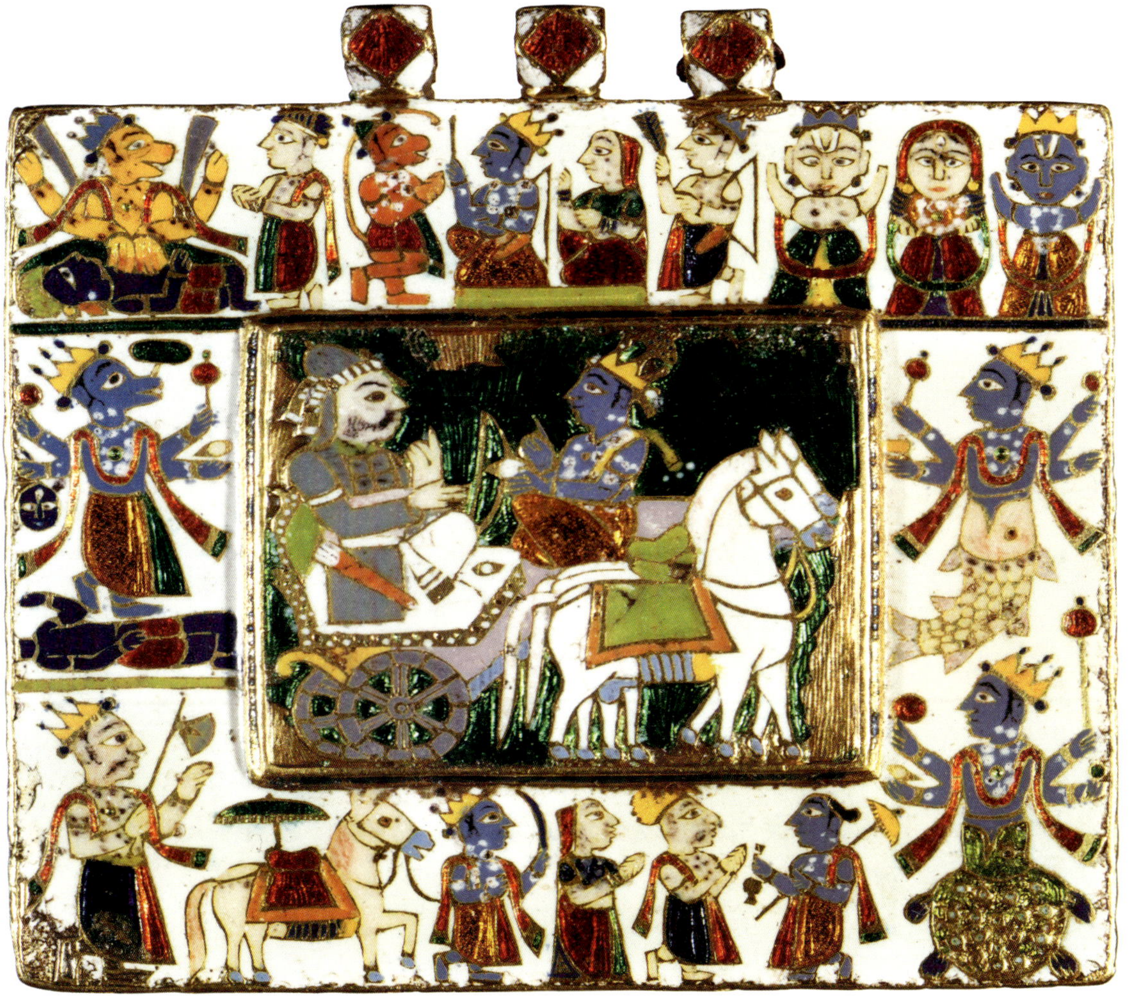

Dashavatara in a minakari locket, Museum of Fine Arts, Boston

and to beautify and adorn that body is a prayer. Beautification with the *solah shringar* or the sixteen adornments or with various jewellery is to assure the body of its nobility and grace. It makes the body *mangalmaya* or auspicious, it protects the body from negative forces and even more it spreads radiance and effulgence all around it."

Adornment is a very special part of the woman who is getting ready to meet her beloved. Helped by her friends, who hold a mirror up to her, she looks at various cosmetics and unguents and makes a final check in the mirror. It is in this mirror that she will see the face of her beloved and when their eyes meet, she will offer all her adornments to him.

It was time to leave and Megha thanked everyone at the store and folding her hands gave them her beaming smile. Then, she along with Vishwakarma walked towards the chariot.

"Rajasthan is full of beautiful handicrafts but I want you to visit Pratap Singh in Udaipur. He makes kathputlis and along with his wife performs shows," Vishwakarma told Megha as the chariot took to the air. On reaching Udaipur,

Megha and Vishwakarma walked towards the house of Pratap Singh. He and his wife welcomed Vishwakarma and Megha and took them to the terrace of their house where half-finished kathputlis were kept. As the family was gathering on the terrace Vishwakarma spoke to Megha. "Patronised by the raja and the *praja* through the ages, puppet plays have been vehicles both for entertainment and religious instruction and in modern India for political messages as well. All puppeteers trace their origin to the Rajput *bhats* who hail from Marwar. The origin of kathputli can be traced back to the throne of the eighth-century king Vikramaditya, called Sinhasan Battisi. It is said that the thirty-two figures carved upon this throne would come alive every night to sing, dance and perform acrobatic feats. The *bhats* are said to have evolved puppetry from these thirty-two characters to create a play based on the life and times of Vikramaditya. This remained the foundation of puppetry for centuries until

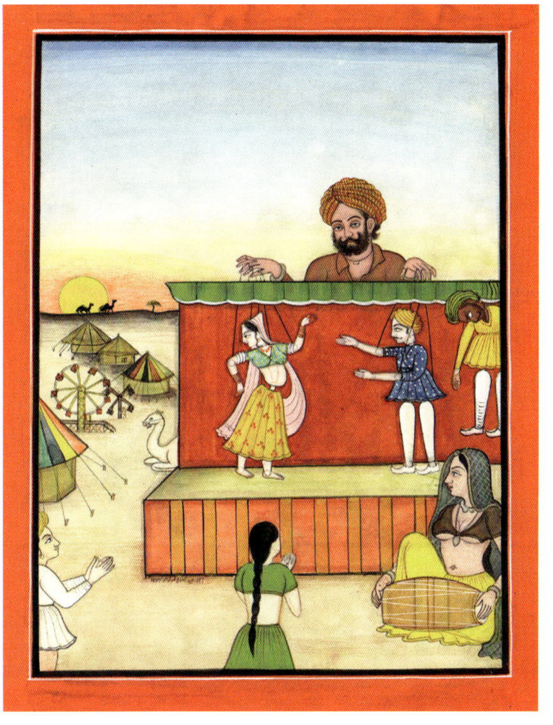

Prithviraj Chauhan inspired the *bhats* to create a story around him. This was then replaced by a play about Amar Singh Rathore. Akbar too patronised puppeteers.

"The traditional stage is simple. Two charpoys borrowed from a neighbouring household form

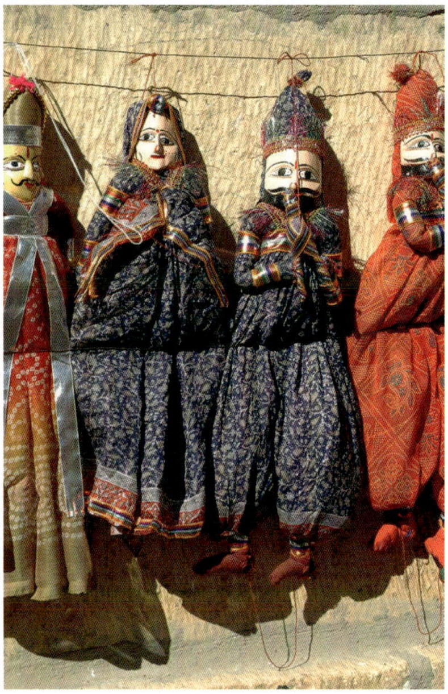

the stage. Light effects are also very basic consisting of a couple of kerosene lamps. During the show the puppeteer speaks the part of the characters and comments on them in a squealing voice with a bamboo whistle placed in his mouth. His wife plays the dholak. The *bhats* believe that the kathputlis are benign celestial beings who not only provide them their livelihood but who come to their aid in times of need. The *bhats* never throw away or sell their kathputlis but instead pass them down the generations. When they are old and broken, they are immersed in holy rivers with rituals. Kathputlis and their performances are an important part of popular theatre in India even today."

Back in the chariot Vishwakarma spoke to Megha:

"I sure you must be tired by now and we should head back to Delhi." Though Megha was eager to learn more, she conceded and they were back in Dilli Haat. The Haat was still full of people milling around. Vishwakarma took Megha by the arm and the two of them sat under a pipal tree.

"I have enjoyed taking you around India to show you some of its craft traditions. Every province and region, every village and town, every family and community has its own unique craft practices and they are all very beautiful, and so are the people who make them. They are all a part of my family."

Vishwakarma continued:

"You must have observed that many craft objects have multiple patterns and adornments. Tied as the Indian mind is to the world of nature, we choose vegetative rather than geometric or abstract motifs in the various adornments. The tree and the creeper, the flower and the blossom, birds and animals, the river and the rain, with which the craftsmen and women associate in their daily activities, become motifs of adornment. Craft is a product of the earth and

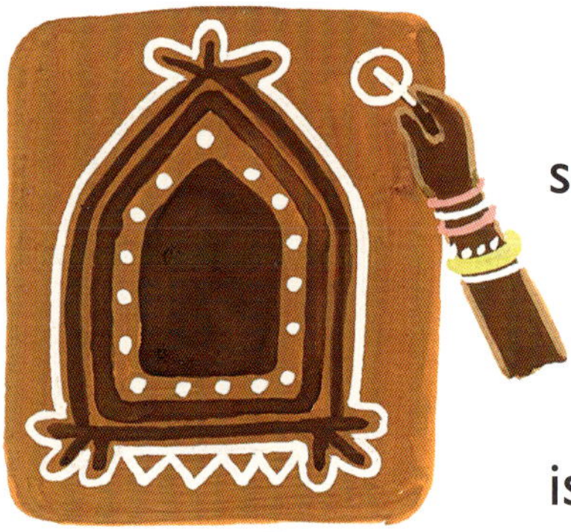

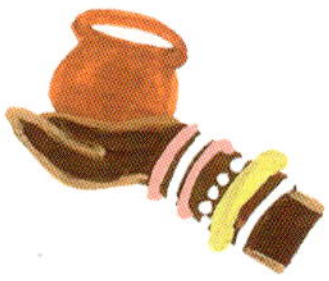

so are the craftspeople and to the earth they remain tied. It is to nature that they return for rest and refuge, inspiration and ideas and they never forget that it is from the womb of the earth that they have risen. It is in a handful of earth that they hear the footfalls of their ancestors and it is the earth and its manifestations that give form to their vision and feelings and creates and sustains the beautiful craft objects that they create. You must remember that handicrafts are valuable not merely as beautiful heritage but because we need to live with them, touch them, feel them, use them and have intimate communion with them so that our life is enriched by their grace. The creation of crafts is a timeless tradition and craftsmen trace their origin to me.

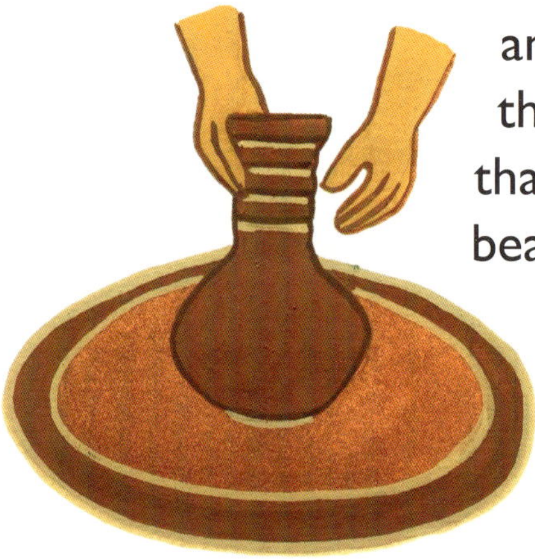

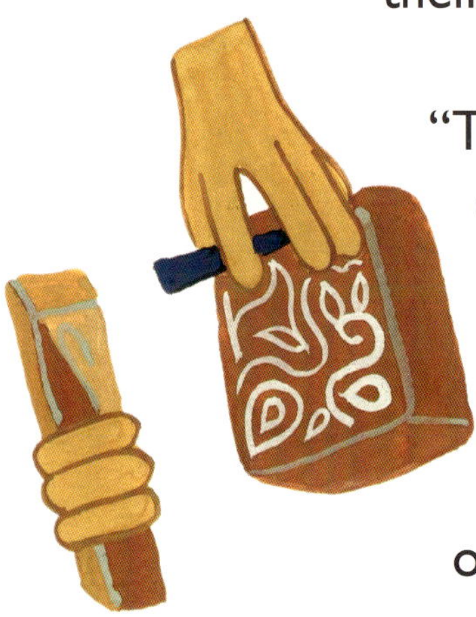

"Through the hands of the craftsman the common becomes cherished, joy giving. Ordinary utilitarian articles like cooking utensils and the toilet box, toys and lamps, clothes and coverings are made beautiful. Craftsmanship is an indigenous creation of the ordinary people to meet their direct human needs and in this sense the craftsperson is also an artist. The only difference being that the crafts were for use by the family and not for commercial purposes. The making of beautiful daily objects was considered a noble act. But as society changed and communities grew in size, the making of crafts became a profession and craftsmen lived and worked in *srenis* or guilds. Young craftsmen were trained in the family and when the demand for crafts increased, young craftsmen were trained in the guru-shishya tradition. In a craft oriented society a master craftsman was also a social leader and was sometimes called the *sutradhar.*"

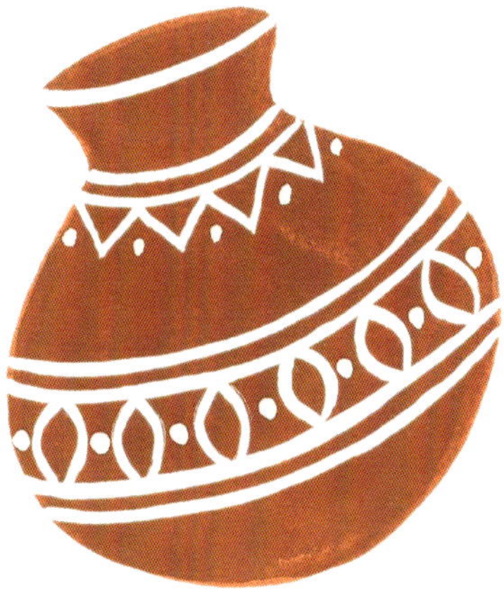

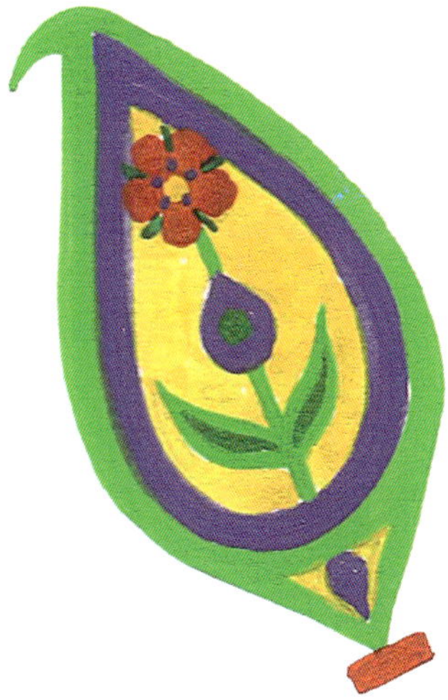

Megha was listening intently to him.

"Did you notice that the beautiful crafts of India which we just saw bridge the gap between Hindus and Muslims? Colours and sounds, textures and shapes, the blossoms and the birds and everything beautiful that human hands create are above religion and caste, colour and creed. The creation and the enjoyment

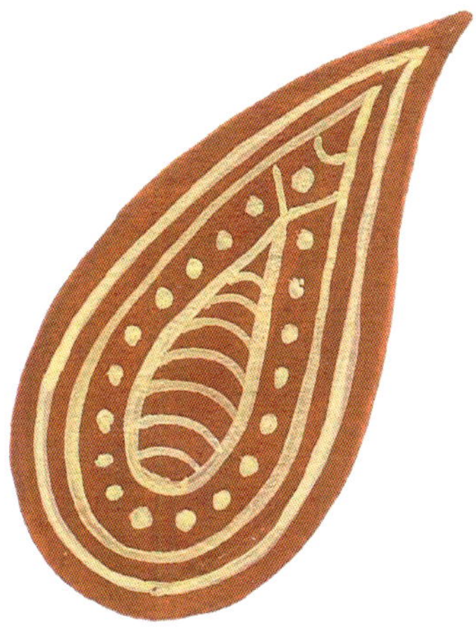

of crafts is like a religion in itself. Craft objects teach us that what is beautiful knows no religion."

Vishwakarma raised his hand and pointing with his finger continued:

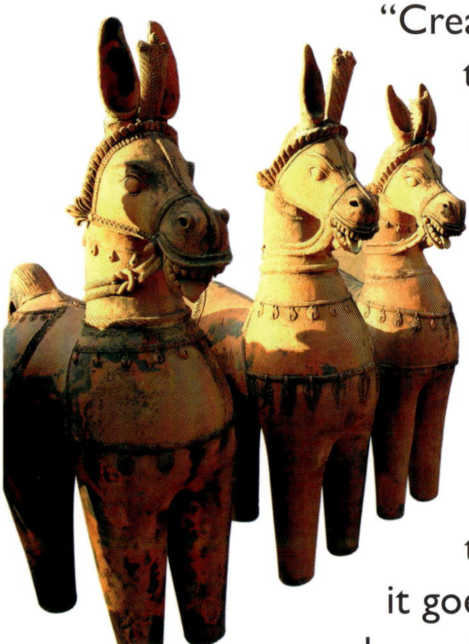

"Creating objects of beauty and giving them centrality in our homes and lives points out the importance of bringing grace and dignity into our lived lives, but it does not stop there. We beautify our surroundings with crafts and thereby bring a certain elegance and brightness into our homes but there's more to it than that; we decorate our living spaces to give them grace and panache but it goes beyond that; we adorn our own selves with the traditional sixteen adornments but there is a higher purpose to creating beauty than mere adornment, decoration or vanity. To be in the midst of the beautiful is to be assured of ancient racial memories and hoary archetypal symbols, of living myths and timeless metaphors, of well-loved designs and traditional patterns, of evocative colours and cosmic shapes. It works

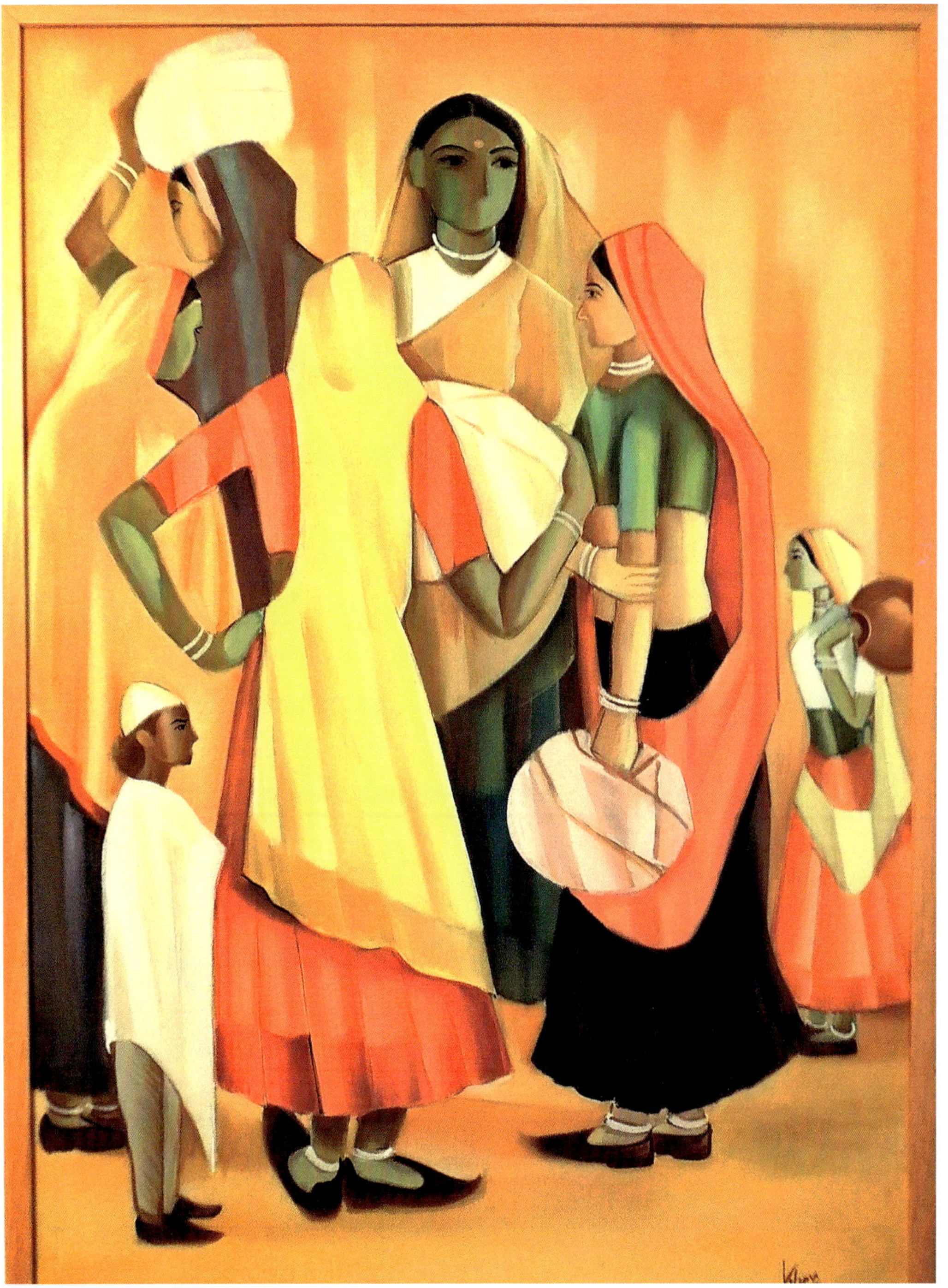

A craft family, painting by Harish Raut

on us at many different levels—magical, religious and aesthetic—assuring us of dignity and well-being."

Vishwakarma's face was animated as he was talking and Megha listened with rapt attention.

"The potter's wheel, the needle of the embroiderer, the mould of the textile block-printer, the brush of the kalamkari maker, the chisel of the sculptor, the kalam of the calligrapher, the spindle of the weaver, the adept hands of the flower-seller making garlands, the tender hands of a young girl learning the first steps of handling cow dung and the bare hands of the housewife making rangolis; these are the basic tools of *akritis* and are a testament to human creativity. In them resides knowledge, an ancient memory, a beautiful energy. In them are bodily rhythms of trackless generations, from their movement will arise metaphors and motifs passed down from mother to daughter and above all, in these hands is the living and pulsating desire to create a beautiful object. And when two hands come together, they will fashion a pot and create an enclosed space which will be filled with water and it will sustain life.

"From these hands will come objects that are both functional and beautiful at the same time, making it hard to decide where function ends and beauty begins, since in these objects is a constant interplay between utility and beauty. These are not symbols nor are they art objects but they have a presence of their own, as if to say 'I am'. They live in connivance and in harmony with our senses, they make no apology for their unabashed sensuality for they do not obey laws of the market-place or dictates of the intellect. We will touch and caress and smell these objects, wonder and admire their evocative shape, adorn our bodies and our homes with them. We will use them in our lived lives and they will give us visual delight as our eyes will be drawn to them and we will lose ourselves in their patterns and textures, their forms and shapes, their colours and hues, and in them we will hear hushed sounds of the moving fingers of craftsmen and women and we will discover hidden truths about life and living. These handcrafted objects will pulsate with the heartbeat of human creativity and move with

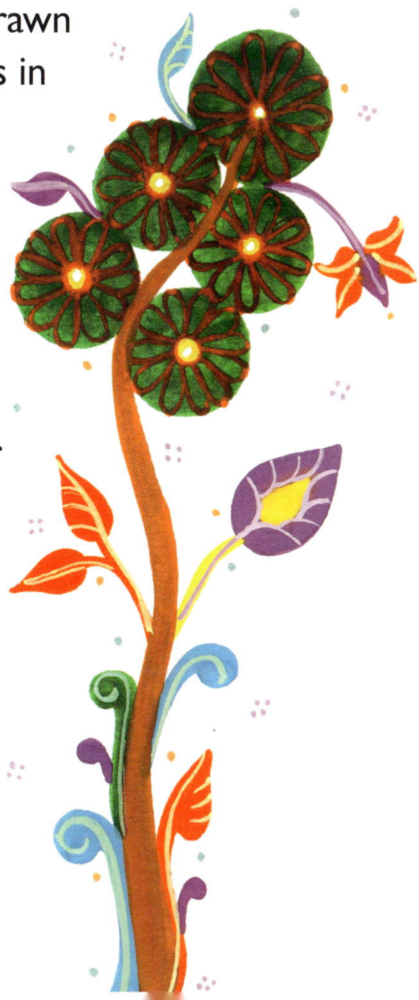

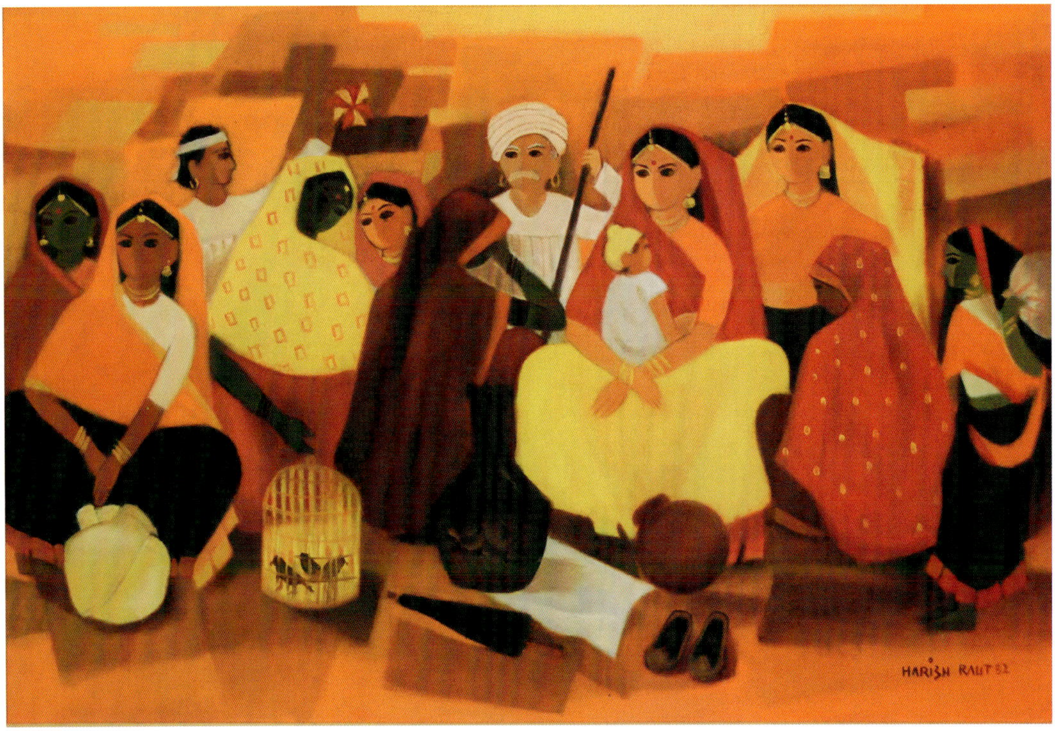

A craft family, painting by Harish Raut

the lifebreath of human imagination. And when we are touched by them we will raise our hands and try to touch the sky, for after all our hands are not for locomotion as they are in animals but have been given to us to express ourselves, our joys and aspirations and dreams and wishes to create beautiful objects."

A group of young women like Megha had gathered and were listening to Vishwakarma.

"You all are bright young women or *nari* but I want you to be a *purna nari*, the complete woman. Do you know what it means?" he asked. Since no one answered Vishwakarma said: "Let me tell you who a *purna nari* is."

"You have probably heard of a *purna kumbha* but a *purna nari* is one who combines in her both *purusha* and prakriti. Prakriti is the earth, matter, soil, the womb, all of which contain our seeds and our rivers, which ensure growth and fertility. It causes plants to grow and trees to bloom, the *kumbhar* to create the pot and the *rangrez* to create beautiful colours. Prakriti is in the movement of the hands which creates all these beautiful craft objects. But prakriti by itself is incomplete. It needs to blend with *purusha*. *Purusha* is the sky, the vastness of space which holds the sun and the moon, it is the akasha towards which trees grow, it is the whisper of joyous abandon which resonates from craft objects. They tell us that utility or just being *sundar* or beautiful is not enough but we must strive for *saundarya* or beauty, which is the sense of ananda within ourselves. Prakriti and *purusha*, matter and spirit, must come together like the *ardhanari*. That is the message of these craft objects. Be therefore an *ardhanari* and that will make you a *purna nari*."

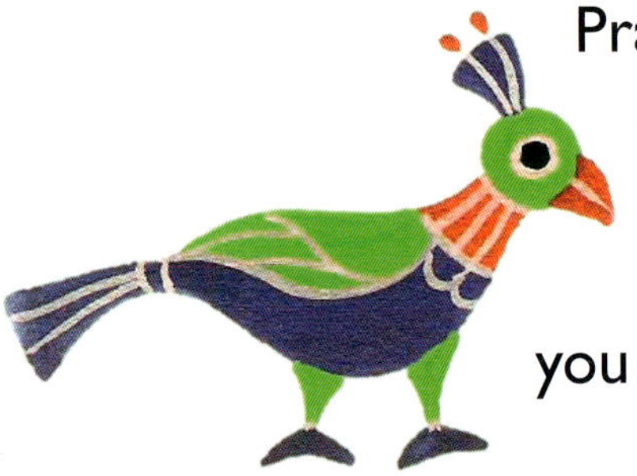

Vishwakarma held up the palms of his hand and said:

"It is our hands that are the main source of creation. The hand is central in any artistic creation and even the word *akriti* incorporates the word *kar*, which means the hand, suggesting that the hand is the main tool of human artistic creativity. Evolutionary biologists pay great attention to the detached thumb and hence its prehensile ability to hold objects, such as weapons and the brush, the pen and the chisel,

and this is the key to human creativity.
A common morning prayer for us is:

Lakshmi resides at the tip of my hand
and Saraswati in the middle
at the bottom of the hand is Govinda
and this morning I venerate that hand."

॥ कराग्रे वसते लक्ष्मी करमध्ये सरस्वती
करमूलेच तु गोविंदं प्रभाते कर दर्शनम् ॥

Just then a leaf from the pipal tree fell into Megha's lap and she felt blessed. She looked around but could not see Vishwakarma. He had disappeared. She was confused but then decided that she just had a beautiful dream.
It was an amazing journey across India that she had undertaken in her dream. It was not the India of temples and monuments, of bazaars and malls, but an India of beauty and its beautiful traditions of arts and crafts, of people who are committed to creating remarkable objects with their hands, of asserting the reality of this world and making it a happy and joyous place.

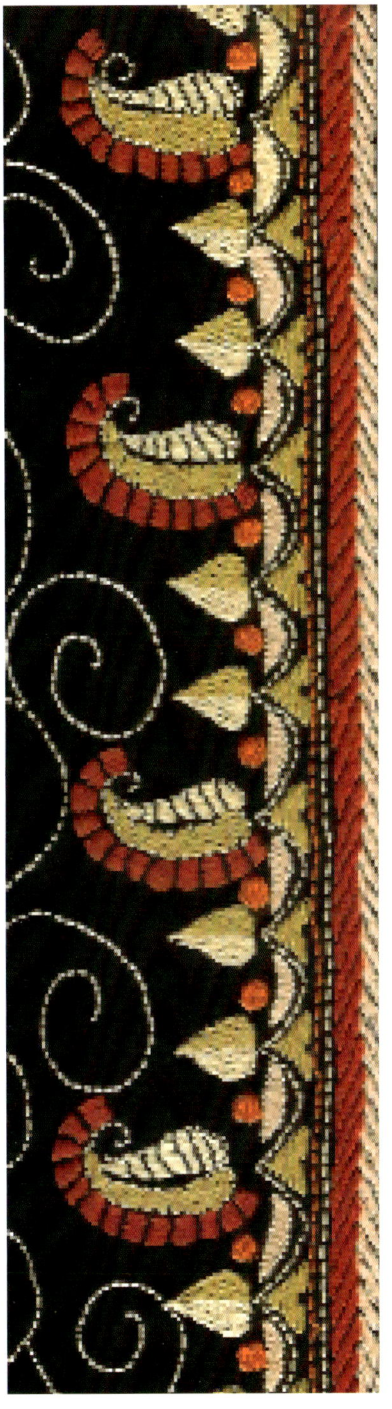

A place where the potter's wheel and the weaver's loom are venerated, where needle and thread are used to give form to their imagination, where colour and texture gives shape to thoughts, where fabric is the canvas upon which they embroider their dreams and wishes, where everything that is lovingly made tells a story, where objects of everyday use are beautifully made and lovingly used and have a honoured place in homes. All the objects that Megha saw had a life of their own, they were alive with feeling and grace. She experienced a bond with these objects and felt connected with the people she met. Megha was a person transformed.

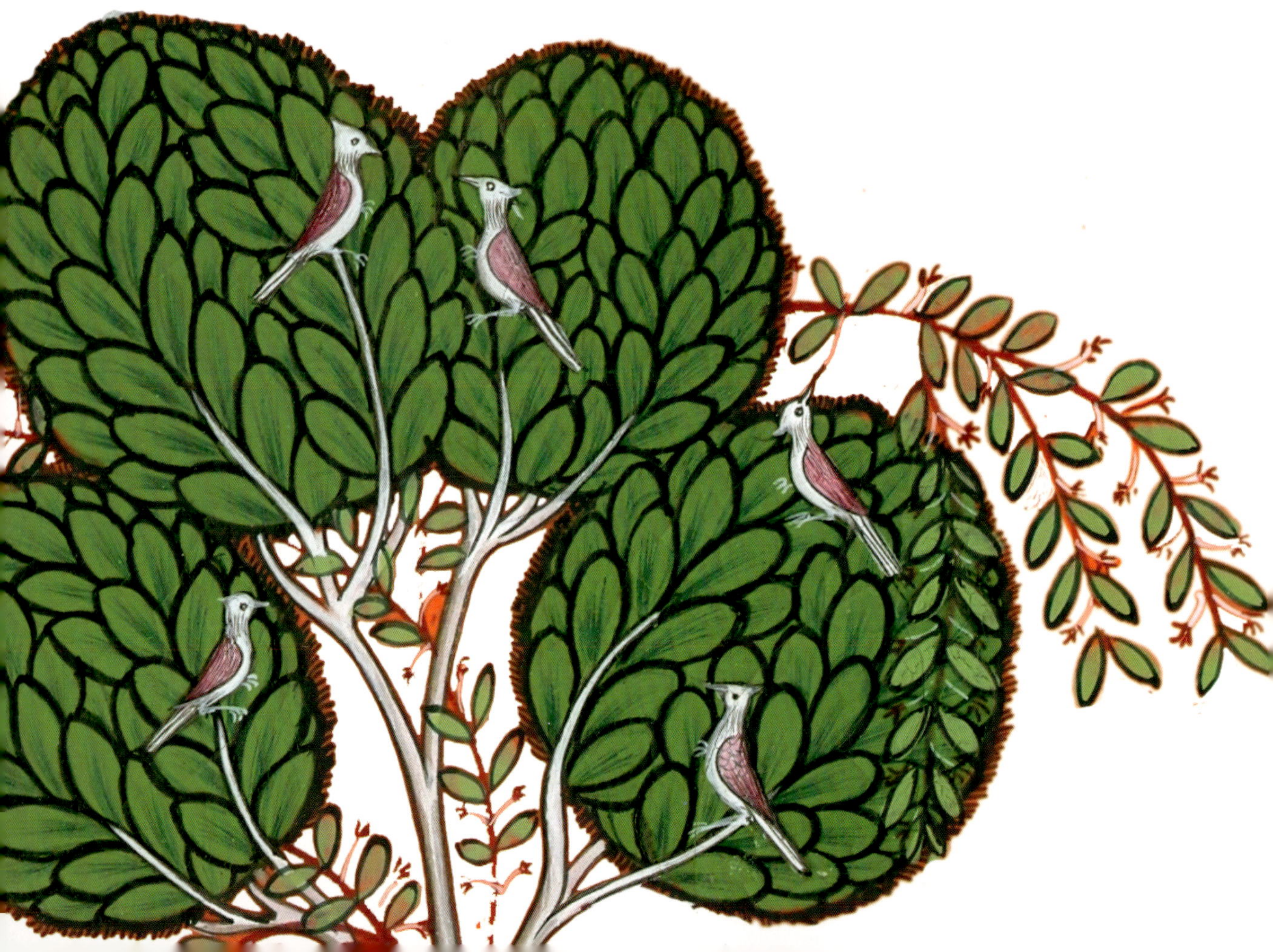

As Megha and her mother went home, she was still clutching on to the pipal leaf and in her mind she relived every moment that she had spent with Vishwakarma and his family of craftspeople. Was it a dream she wondered, and even if it was, she would convert her dream into reality.

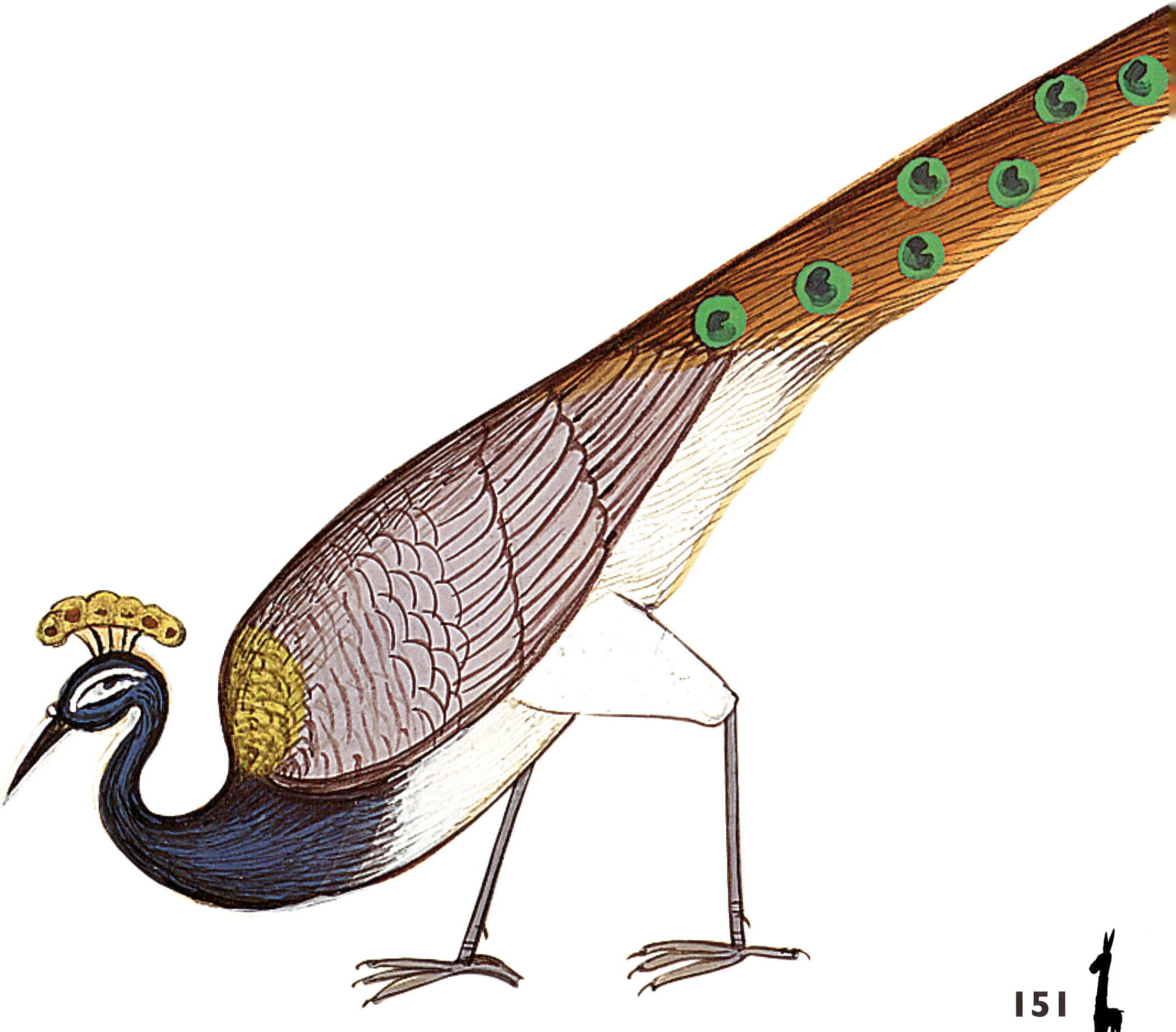

Vidai

While Megha goes back home at the end of this dream journey, our task has just begun; for we must start our own excursion into the romance and magnificence of the crafts. We must abandon the artificial distinction between art and craft and look upon the various handcrafted objects as items of beauty. They are everyday objects of utility yet they possess charm and beauty, they add grace and dignity to our homes, there is a certain reality and truth about them. They seem to say, "I am a part of this beautiful world and so are you." These simple but beautiful objects—the *ghada* and the *ghoda*, shawls and saris, icons and images, *rang* and *rachana*—are all a creation of the human hand and imagination and become a part of our lives. We live with them, touch them, wear them; they find a place in our kitchens and living rooms and even in our temples and havelis. They know no

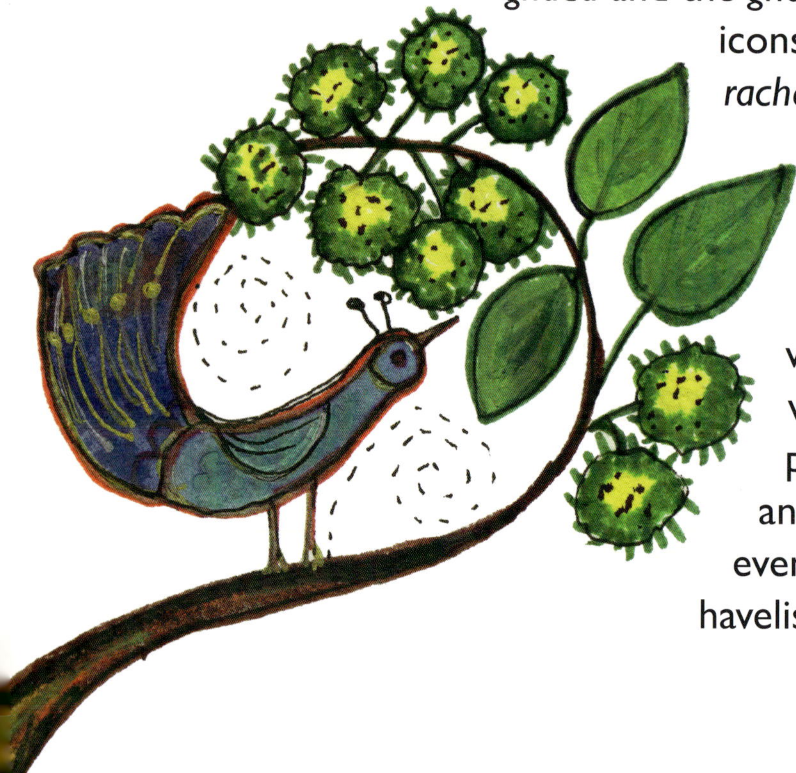

religion or caste, they do not speak any language, they observe no rules, yet they are beautifully Indian and they unite and enrich us. The art of making these objects is passed down from one generation to the next and in this sense they preserve the memory and heritage of the family. In them we see the genius of human creativity, the joy of adornment, the pleasure of making our surroundings pleasant, the excitement of beautifying our everyday life. When we use them it is akin to inviting the potter and the carpenter, the jeweller and the *rangrez* into our homes and respecting their work. The motifs and designs are simple but under the patina of simplicity lies a world view of growth and fertility where living a full and noble life is the goal, where every moment is meant to be auspicious and ennobling.

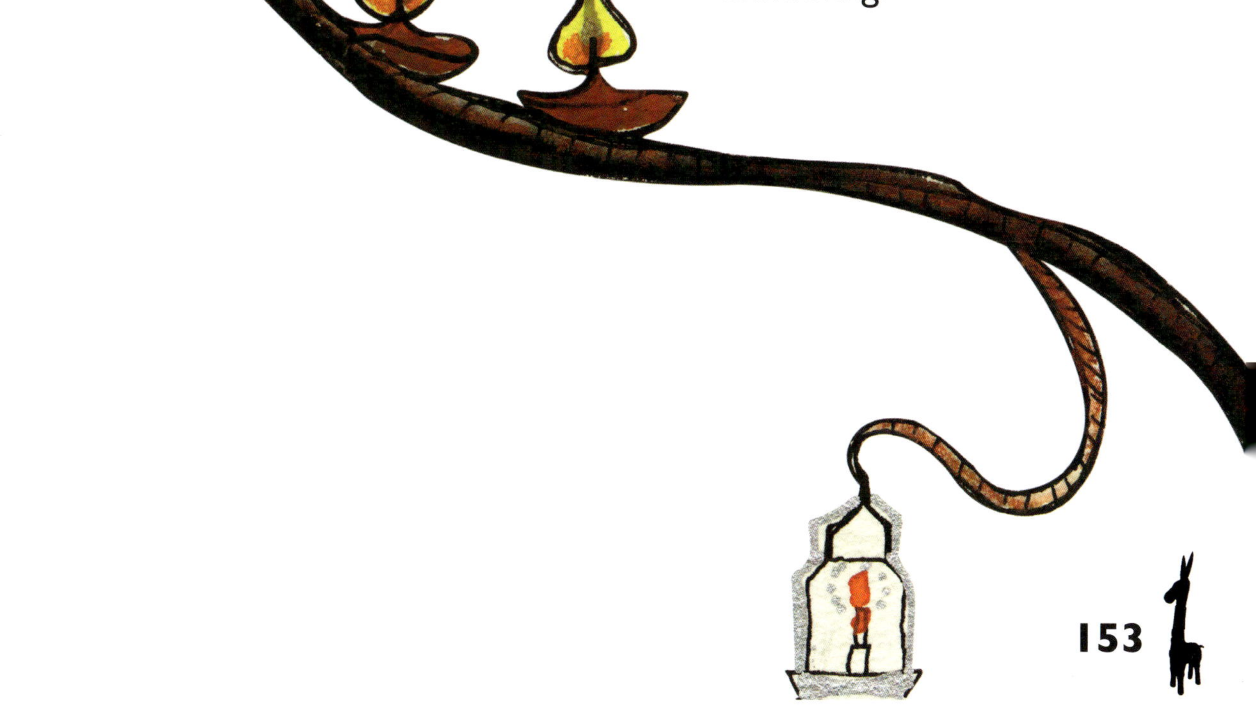

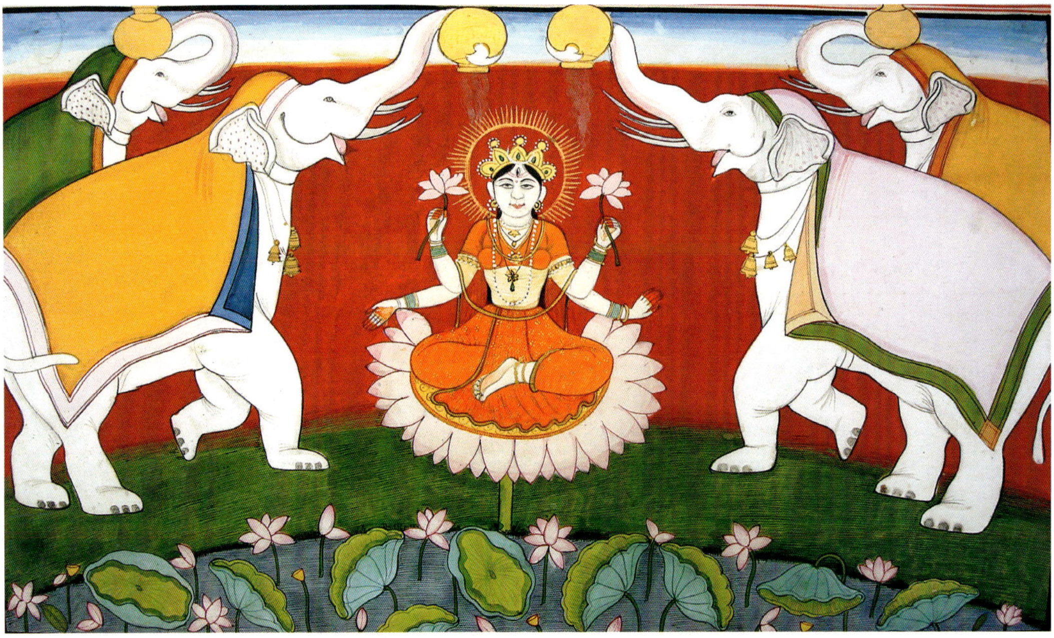

Gajalakshmi, painting by Vijay Sharma

These objects recognise woman as the original creator, the Adi Shakti, the *garbha* where beauty is born, the woman who spins and spreads the threads of creation. In her is alive the wisdom of *srishti* or creation and the throb of prakriti or matter. Through the drawing of rangoli or making of toys from mother earth she holds the family joyously together. There is something sacred about these craft objects not because they are meant for gods and goddesses, nor because they are sanctioned by priests or patrons, but because they are expressions of human creativity and indicators of an integrated and full life, where life and living, art and craft, utility and beauty are an organic whole. Let us touch the earth for in it are the footfalls and voices of our ancestors who first created these objects.

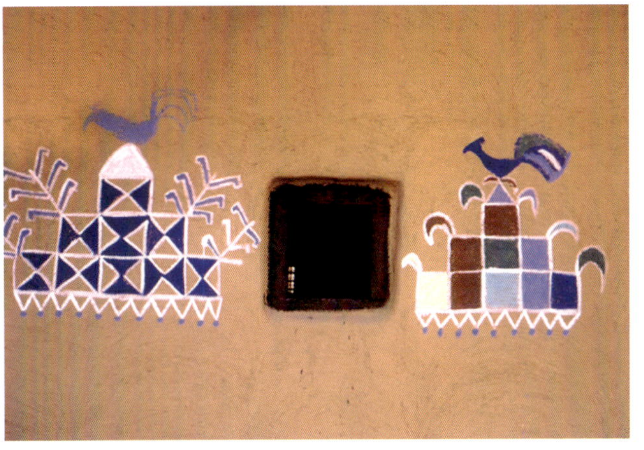

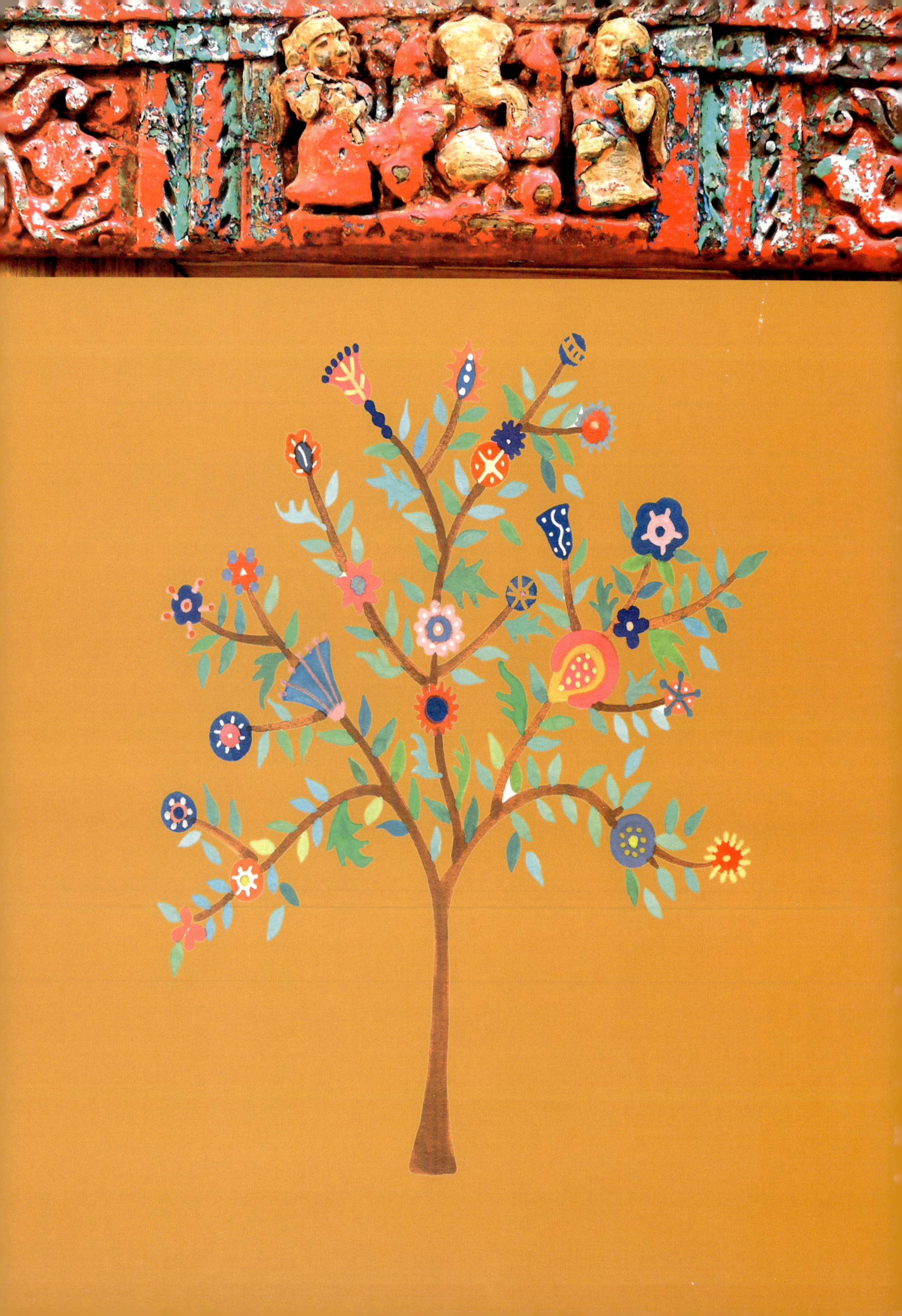

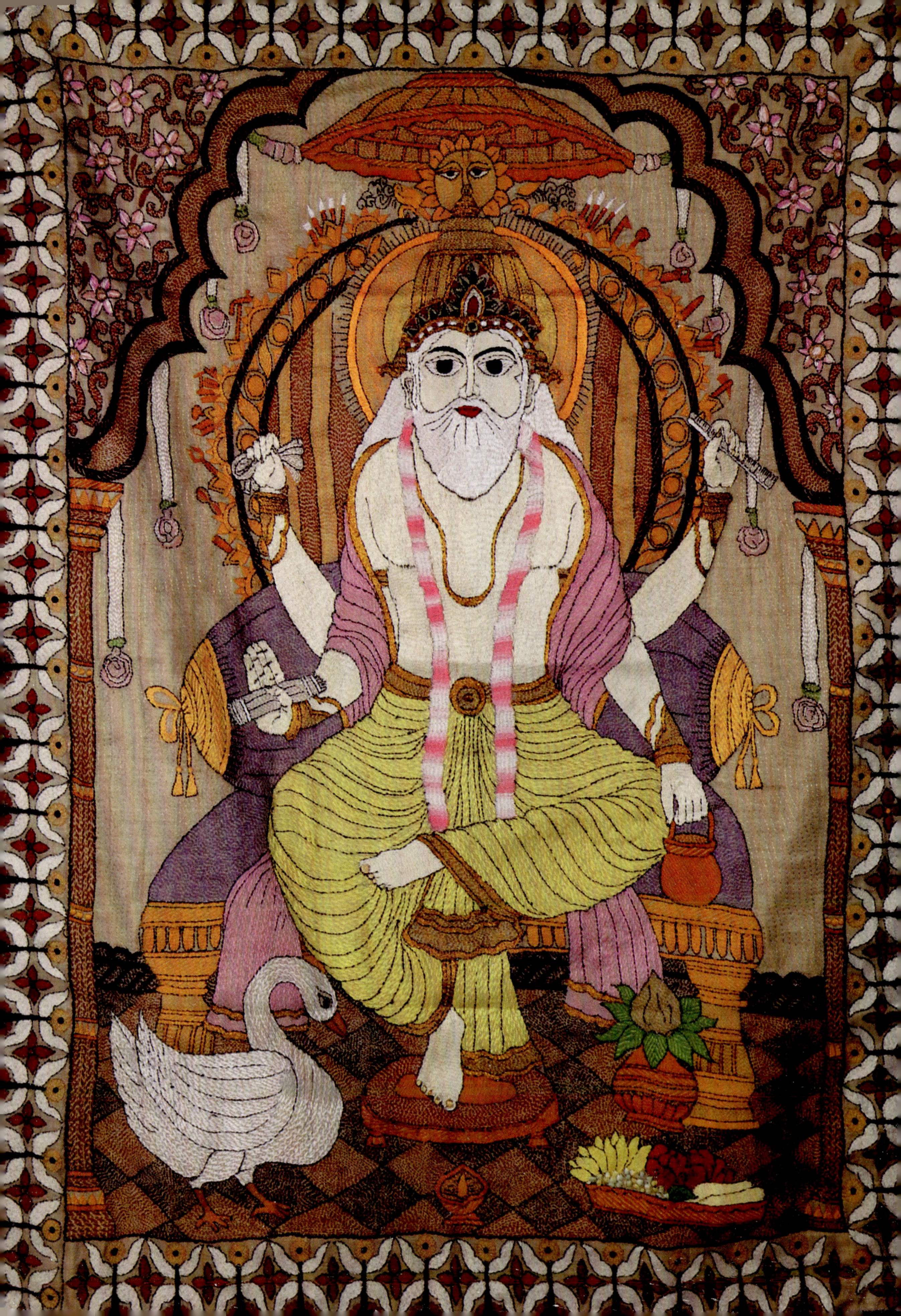